Listening In & Speaking Out

Sharon Bode
Charles G. Whitley
Gary James

Longman

New York

LISTENING IN AND SPEAKING OUT
ADVANCED

ISBN 0 582 79737 3

First printing 1981

5   4

Sponsoring Editor: Larry Anger
Project Editor: Joanne Dresner
Illustrations: Anna Veltfort
Cover Design: Frederick Charles Ltd.
Design: Antler and Baldwin Inc.

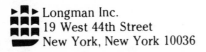Longman Inc.
19 West 44th Street
New York, New York 10036

Distributed in the United Kingdom by Longman Group Ltd., Longman House, Burnt Mill, Harlow, Essex CM20 2JE, England, and by associated companies branches and representatives throughout the world.

Printed in the U.S.A.

To the teachers who taught us the most:

RUTH CRYMES

INA MILLER

TED PLAISTER

and

To the students of the Kyoto YMCA English School

ACKNOWLEDGEMENTS

Over the years countless people have been involved in assisting us to bring these materials to their present form. We gratefully acknowledge their help and express our appreciation to:

Bette Matthews, who is the marvelous fourth voice in the dramatizations;

the entire Kyoto YMCA English School teaching staff, especially Kiyo Inagaki and Ray Mori, for their splendid support;

the administration of the Kyoto YMCA English School, including Yoshiyuki Kuroda, Shinichi Mitani, Yoshihiro Sakai, Taiichi Takaya and Seisuke Ue, for their faith in our efforts;

the office staff of the Kyoto YMCA English School, especially Toshiko Fujiwara, Takako Hata Itahara and Machiko Morimoto, for their devoted labors;

Akira Ogawa of Sangyo Daigaku and Katsumi Ige and his staff of Honolulu Community College, for their fine technical assistance in recording the materials;

Yutaka Akimaru and Tadashi Inoue, who made it possible to get earlier versions of the materials duplicated;

Susie Young and Robert Dilley of the American Language Institute, University of Southern California, for their willing assistance in duplicating tapes;

Al Hoel and Sharyn Klafehn, for their belief in the materials and their encouragement;

Clara Iwata, Kathy Langaman, Adela Rhoades and Arlene Yano of Honolulu Community College and Evangeline Colbero and Eleanor Curry of Chaminade University of Honolulu, for their excellent typing;

Bill Wiley and Lou Willand of Honolulu Community College and Eleanor Frierson of Chaminade University of Honolulu, for providing an academic atmosphere that has allowed these materials to flourish;

and Joanne Dresner of Longman Inc. for her interest and editorial assistance.

CONTENTS

INTRODUCTION

LISTENING IN AND SPEAKING OUT focuses on spontaneous spoken English with the aim of bridging the gap between "classroom English" and the English that students are likely to encounter on their own. The activities are based on two kinds of recordings made by native speakers of English from various regions of the United States. The first recording in each unit is an unscripted, unrehearsed Monolog which lasts approximately one minute. Each speaker describes a past experience or relates an anecdote in an informal manner, as if speaking to friends. The second recording in each unit is an unrehearsed Dramatization, also unscripted to ensure spontaneity, which lasts approximately a minute and a half. It incorporates some element of conflict or disagreement in order to expose students to expressions of strong feelings and to provide them with an opportunity to discuss a variety of emotional responses.

Because the language on the recordings was unrehearsed and the interactions were spontaneous, the learners will hear many instances of natural hesitations, interruptions, parenthetical expressions, unfinished sentences and awkward or "incorrect" grammatical constructions. Sometimes they will hear very rapid speech and at other times slower rates of delivery.

Through exposure to the ordinary phenomena of spoken English in LISO, learners are given the opportunity to develop the skill of understanding real conversations in English spoken at normal speed. In addition, the material provides: 1) an opportunity for students to speak informally; 2) a learning environment that is student-centered; and 3) activities that help students develop the confidence, motivation and ideas for on-going self-instruction.

DESCRIPTION OF THE ACTIVITIES AND SUGGESTIONS FOR THEIR USE

LISTENING IN AND SPEAKING OUT, ADVANCED can be used as the primary text in a listening comprehension class or as a supplementary text. It is not necessary to start with Unit One and go through the material in order; because the recorded material is totally unscripted, there is no vocabulary or structure control.

Tuning In. Vocabulary items likely to be unfamiliar to advanced-level students have been defined according to the context in the recordings. However, words that may be new but are not essential to the main idea of the Monolog or Dramatization have not been defined in order to encourage students to use context to aid comprehension and not simply decode vocabulary items. Before students listen to the recording, it is helpful to provide examples of the new words in sentences and have students create their own sentences. In addition to familiarizing students with the new language they are about to hear, this prelistening activity serves to introduce them to the topic of the recording.

Sometimes the meaning of a new word or expression may not be fully understood until after students hear the vocabulary in context. For lower-level students the tape can be stopped frequently to focus on the new words. Then vocabulary can be reviewed and practiced as necessary after listening to the recording.

Summing Up. These questions aid comprehension by helping students focus on the important points in the Monolog. Students may read the questions silently or aloud before they listen to the recording. It is important that they understand the questions so they will be able to focus on the information as they listen. Then students close their books while they listen to the Monolog. The recording may be played as many times as necessary until students feel comfortable that they have grasped the general content. Finally they answer the comprehension questions, orally or in writing. Answers can be discussed either in small groups or as a class. The correct responses can be found in the Answer Key.

Retelling. Students have an opportunity to give their own version of the Monolog, orally or in writing. They may follow the phrases provided in the text but should be encouraged to paraphrase the Monolog on their own if possible. Students can take turns retelling the Monolog to the whole class, they can work in small groups (with one person following the Tapescript to help the others if necessary), or they can work in pairs. For small groups or pairs, the teacher moves around the class, providing assistance when requested by students. The teacher should refrain from correcting students' grammar or pronunciation during the retelling in order to encourage them to express the ideas they heard and to develop confidence in speaking.

Filling In. This exercise, which can be used as a test, is a cloze activity based on the transcription of the recorded material. By now students have heard the recording several times and should be familiar enough with the content to focus on specific words. They fill in the blanks as they listen to the recording. Students with experience in intensive listening should be able to do very well; those who haven't will usually need more guidance and will score lower at first.

The following is a suggested procedure for the exercise: The teacher plays the Monolog or Dramatization straight through while students read along as they listen. Then the tape is rewound and played until just past the first blank; using the instant stop or pause button, the teacher allows enough time to write the word. For more advanced students the tape can be stopped after longer segments of speech. Before students' answers are checked, the entire recorded text should be played through again. They can check their own exercises by comparing their answers with the Tapescript. They should circle their errors *without* writing the correct forms in the blanks. Then, as the recording is played again, students try to correct their errors as they listen. They can check their exercises again with the Tapescript or review the correct forms orally in pairs, small groups or with the whole class.

Speaking Out. Students choose a topic to talk about as the culminating activity for each section of a unit. After focusing on the language of native speakers of English in preceding exercises, they now have an opportunity to practice the communication skills they have learned by interacting with each other in small groups.

For the Monolog activity individuals select topics of interest to present to their groups. It is not necessary for each student to choose a different topic or for all topics to be the same. It is only important for them to speak about something of high interest so that they have a desire to communicate their ideas. They may prepare their monologs for homework or speak extemporaneously. The length of their presentations will vary with individuals, one minute being the average. Just as students paraphrased the recorded Monolog, they should be encouraged to state other students' ideas in their own words. This will increase their motivation to listen and help them check if they have understood each other.

For the Dramatization activity each group decides on a topic of interest to all of the members. The process of choosing a topic can become an interesting speaking activity itself. For homework students write a short paragraph or composition on the topic. The writing exercise will help them organize their ideas for the discussion and assure that each person has something to contribute. When the class meets again, students may read each other's papers to become familiar with other ideas of the group. This will often "break the ice" to begin the discussion.

As in the **Retelling** activity, the teacher can listen to each group by circulating among them, providing assistance when requested by students. The teacher should not interrupt students to correct their speech. They should feel that this activity is an opportunity for them to converse freely in English and to get to know the other people in their group.

Talking It Over. These questions, written to aid comprehension, have been divided into two sections. To answer the first set of questions, students listen for the general idea of the Dramatization. Rather than trying to understand everything they hear the first few times they listen to the recording, students should be encouraged to grasp the mood, setting and relationship among the speakers first. The second set of questions focuses their attention on the important interactions. By answering these questions, they will be able to summarize briefly what happened in the Dramatization. As in the **Summing Up** exercise, it is important that students understand the questions before they hear the recording and close their books while listening. The recording may be played as many times as necessary. Answers can be discussed orally either in small groups or as a class. Possible responses can be found in the Answer Key.

Focusing In. This exercise focuses students' attention on the language forms and functions of specific interactions in the Dramatization. After answering the questions in **Talking It Over,** thus becoming familiar with the content, they should be able to pick out key phrases and discuss their communicative purpose. For students having difficulty taking notes as they listen, the tape can be stopped to give them time to write. It is not always necessary for them to repeat the speakers' exact words, especially when a statement is long. It is more important for students to paraphrase the speakers and then discuss the various forms that can be used to communicate the same function (for example, making an accusation or refusing an invitation). The correct responses or examples of possible responses can be found in the Answer Key.

Taking Part. In this activity students have an opportunity to practice the kinds of interactions they heard in the recorded Dramatization. First they act out their own versions of the recording. Having discussed the various language forms and functions in **Focusing In,** students should not have difficulty using the language they have learned on their own. In the second situation they act out a scene that is entirely different from the recorded Dramatization in content but includes the same kinds of functional interactions.

The following is a suggested procedure for the classroom management of the activity: Divided into groups of three, the class takes a few minutes to prepare their parts. The groups act out the situations simultaneously, while the teacher listens to each group. One group is then asked to perform their dramatization for the class. Students may choose to keep the same partners for the second situation but should be encouraged to interact with different people in subsequent units.

Answer Key. Possible responses for **Summing Up, Talking It Over** and **Focusing In.**

Tapescript. A complete transcription of the recorded Monologs and Dramatizations, with the language written exactly as it was spoken.

HONESTY

MONOLOG

TUNING IN

Study these words if they are new to you.

1. **tell a lie:** say something you know is not true
2. **take advantage of:** use (someone) for your own purposes
3. **dealings:** relations with other people
4. **cheat:** act dishonestly

SUMMING UP

Read these questions before you hear the recording. Then listen to the recording and answer the questions.

1. According to Chuck, what do we often expect of people?

_____

2. Why does Chuck think this expectation might be unfair?

_____

3. What did his friend realize after they got out of the restaurant?

_____

4. What did he do after realizing what had happened?

_____

5. What did Chuck learn from watching his friend?

_____

RETELLING

State the ideas in the monolog in your own words. You can use the phrases below as a guide.

Chuck read in the newspaper the other day that _____

_____ .

He thinks we often expect _____

_____

_____ .

The other day _____

_____

_____ .

He was pleasantly surprised _____ .

FILLING IN

Listen to the recording and fill in the blanks.

I read in the newspaper the other day that we tell between two hundred and three hundred

lies every day. It makes me wonder if _____ is still important.
                                        1

Uh, there're _____ many times when we _____ seem to expect people
               2   3

_____ be dishonest rather than _____ honest. We expect, uh, individuals
  4   5

_____ try to take advantage _____ other people whenever they _____ .
  6   7   8

And we sometimes expect _____, uh, to . . . not always be _____ in their dealings.
                          9   10

And _____ even expect students, sometimes, _____ cheat on exams or, uh,
      11   12

_____ things to help their _____ . I wonder if that's _____ fair to these people.
  13   14   15

_____ I still think there're _____ people.
  16   17

The other day _____ very good friend of _____ and I were in _____
                18   19   20

restaurant. Uh, when the cashier _____ him back, uh, his money, uh, _____ we got
                                   21   22

out of _____ restaurant, he realized that _____ had ten or fifteen _____
          23   24   25

more than he was _____ to have. He didn't _____ hesitate at all. He _____ right
                  26   27   28

back in and _____ it back, and of _____ the cashier was very _____.
            29   30   31

But, uh, I was pleasantly _____, because it means that _____ really are people
                          32   33

running _____ who are honest.
        34

SPEAKING OUT

Choose one of the topics below and make up your own monolog.

1. Describe a personal experience which proved to you that "honesty is the best policy."
2. Describe a personal experience which proved to you that it is sometimes necessary to lie.
3. Report on an experience you had with the police.
4. Tell about any personal experience related to the topic of the monolog.

THAT'S MY MONEY

DRAMATIZATION

TUNING IN

Study these words if they are new to you.

1. **keep track of** (something): know where (something) is
2. **stoop:** bend your body forwards and down

TALKING IT OVER

Read the first three questions. Then listen to the dramatization and answer the questions.

1. How many speakers are there?
2. Are the people friends, relatives or strangers?
3. Where does the conversation take place?

Now read these questions. Then listen to the dramatization again and answer the questions.

4. What are the two women arguing about?
5. According to the second speaker, why was the twenty dollar bill on the ground?
6. When did the first speaker notice that twenty dollars were missing?
7. Where does she think she dropped the money?
8. What is the man trying to do?

FOCUSING IN

Read these questions about the language the speakers use for specific purposes during the dramatization. Listen again, taking notes if you need to. Then discuss your answers to the questions.

1. The first speaker begins by making an accusation. What does she say? How does she begin in order to be polite?

_____

2. The second speaker denies that she has the other woman's money. In your own words, what does she say? What does she say to be polite?

_____

3. What does the man say to enter the conversation?

_____

4. What do you think the woman means when she says, "Oh, now really"? How do you think she feels?

_____

FILLING IN

Listen to the dramatization and fill in the missing words.

1. FIRST WOMAN: Uh, I'm sorry, but I think that's my money you've got.

2. SECOND WOMAN: _____.
                                                    1
                   I was walking into the store, and the wind was rather strong and blew it out of my hand. I'm sorry. You must've

                   _____.
                                                    2

3. FIRST WOMAN: Uh, but, uh, I had forty dollars this morning, and I've only got twenty now, and I had it when I got out of the taxi.

                   _____.
                                                    3

4. SECOND WOMAN: Well, I'm ... I'm sorry that you don't seem to be able to keep track of your money, but ...

5. POLICEMAN: Excuse me.

_____.
                                              4

6. SECOND WOMAN: I'm sorry. This lady thinks that this is her money, and I've just dropped
                        it and picked it up, and

_____,
                                              5

                        I'll just be on my way.

7. FIRST WOMAN: I know it's my money.

8. POLICEMAN: Uh ...

9. FIRST WOMAN: I mean, I came out, and she ... she had it in her hand.

_____.
                                              6

10. POLICEMAN: Well, don't get excited. Let's just talk about it for a minute. You have
                        the money. When did you pick up the money?

_____?
                                              7

11. SECOND WOMAN: Well, I didn't find the money. I just dropped it.

_____,
                                              8

                        and I opened my wallet to pay the taxi driver, and the wind blew
                        the twenty dollar bill onto the ground, and I just stooped to pick it up,
                        and

_____
                                              9

                        that somebody had lost it and tried to get it first, but actually ...

12. POLICEMAN: I see. I see.

13. FIRST WOMAN: But ... (sigh)

14. POLICEMAN: What makes you think that was yours?

15. FIRST WOMAN: I had ... I had forty dollars in my pocketbook just a minute ago. I just
                        went into the store, and

_____,
                                             10

                        I noticed that twenty dollars was gone, and I came out, and here ...
                        here it was on the ground just as she started to pick it up.

16. POLICEMAN: _____
                                             11

                        your money inside the department store?

17. FIRST WOMAN: I don't think so.

18. SECOND WOMAN: I think that you must have, because I just ...

19. FIRST WOMAN: I mean I found it on the sidewalk. I mean it was right there when she ...
                        was trying to pick it up.

20. SECOND WOMAN: Actually it was my money that you found because

---
¹²

out of my purse when I tried to pay the taxi driver.

21. FIRST WOMAN: Oh, now really!

TAKING PART

Choose two partners and act out the situations below.

Situation One

Background: Two people are arguing about a twenty dollar bill.

SPEAKER #1 You just saw someone pick up a twenty dollar bill outside of a department store, and you are sure it is yours. Accuse the person of picking up your money.

SPEAKER #2 You have just picked up a twenty dollar bill that you think you have dropped. Another person claims that the money is his/hers. Deny that you picked up this person's money.

SPEAKER #3 You are a policeman, and you hear two people arguing in front of a store. Try to calm them down and find out what the problem is.

Situation Two

Background: Two people are arguing about a seat on a crowded bus.

SPEAKER #1 You have been standing on a crowded bus for some time. You are tired, and your arms ache from carrying a heavy package. The person in front of you is preparing to leave. As you move to allow the person to get up, someone pushes you aside and takes your seat. Accuse that person of "stealing" your place.

SPEAKER #2 You have just gotten on a crowded bus and have been lucky enough to find a seat. Just as you sit down, someone starts shouting at you, claiming that you have taken his/her seat. Deny that you have taken this person's seat.

SPEAKER #3 You are seated on a crowded bus next to two people who are arguing about a seat. You cannot avoid becoming involved. Try to calm them down and suggest a solution.

SPEAKING OUT

Read the discussion topics below and choose one to talk or write about.

1. In the dramatization the two women started to argue over who had dropped the money. Have you ever argued with a stranger? Describe the situation and how you felt about it.

2. Have you ever found or lost anything that was valuable? How did you feel? Discuss whether or not you believe in the saying "Finders keepers."

3. Choose your own discussion topic related to the dramatization.

MAKING DECISIONS

MONOLOG

TUNING IN

Study these words if they are new to you.

1. *ponder:* think deeply about
2. *responsibility:* something or someone to take care of
3. *allow:* let (someone) do something
4. *consult with* (someone): ask (someone) for advice

SUMMING UP

Read these questions before you hear the recording. Then listen to the recording and answer the questions.

1. What can some of Gary's friends do more easily than his other friends?

_____

2. What has he noticed about his sister's children?

_____

3. Why does he think they have this ability?

_____

4. What does his sister allow the children to do?

_____

5. Why does Gary think some of his friends can't make decisions easily?

_____

RETELLING

State the ideas in the monolog in your own words. You can use the phrases below as a guide.

Some of Gary's friends can _____

_____

_____.

His sister's children _____.

He thinks one of the reasons _____

_____

_____.

Some of his friends _____.

Maybe their parents _____.

FILLING IN

Listen to the recording and fill in the blanks.

It's amusing to me to watch some of my friends who can come to a decision **right away, and** then some others who can't. Some people can look _____ a menu, can pick _____ a

1   2

menu and right _____ know what they're going _____ have for dinner that

3   4

_____. Then others will ponder _____ look at the thing _____ not be able to

5   6   7

_____ any kind of a _____ for a long, long _____ without some help.

8   9   10

I _____ thinking about this when _____ was talking to my _____ the other

11   12   13

day, and _____ thought about her children, uh, _____ they come to decisions.

14   15

_____ seems to me that _____ young children they come _____ decisions

16   17   18

very quickly, and _____ was thinking about this, _____ I . . . one of the _____

19   20   21

might be that she _____ given them a great _____ of responsibility at a

22   23

_____ young age. She has _____ them to make decisions _____ their own. She

24   25   26

takes _____ shopping many times, and _____ allows them to choose _____ of

27   28   29

their own liking, _____ I think in a _____ this teaches a great _____ of

30   31   32

responsibility. Uh, of course, _____ consult with her sometimes, _____, uh, many
                                    33   34
times they're able _____ decide on something on _____ own, and I was
                        35   36
_____ about my friends and _____ they were ... some of _____ were not able
      37   38   39
to _____ a decision on their _____ and maybe their parents _____ allow them
      40   41   42
to decide _____ something, decide on clothes.
              43

SPEAKING OUT

Choose one of the topics below and make up your own monolog.

1. Describe a difficult decision you once had to make.
2. Tell about a time when you followed another person's advice and regretted doing so.
3. Discuss a decision you made which your family disapproved of.
4. Tell about any personal experience related to the topic of the monolog.

LET'S GO OUT AND CELEBRATE

DRAMATIZATION

TUNING IN

Study these words if they are new to you.

1. *take* (time) *off:* spend (time) away from work
2. *call in:* report (being absent or late) by telephone
3. *show up:* be present
4. *It's my treat:* I'll pay for everything

TALKING IT OVER

Read the first three questions. Then listen to the dramatization and answer the questions.

1. Are the people friends or strangers?
2. Do they have jobs or are they students?
3. What do two of them want to do?

Now read these questions. Then listen to the dramatization again and answer the questions.

4. Why is Bette excited?

5. Chuck gives three reasons why he can't go out. What are they?

6. How did Sharon and Bette describe the place they want to go?

7. How do they convince Chuck that money isn't a problem?

FOCUSING IN

Read these questions about the language the speakers use for specific purposes during the dramatization. Listen again, taking notes if you need to. Then discuss your answers to the questions.

1. Bette is very excited when she asks her friends to go out with her. In your own words, what does she say?

   _____

2. Chuck tries to be polite in refusing Bette's invitation. How does he begin his response?

   _____

3. What do you think Chuck means when he says, "There's a little thing about money"?

   _____

4. Chuck makes a suggestion to try to end the discussion. What does he say?

   _____

FILLING IN

Listen to the dramatization and fill in the missing words.

1. BETTE: Gee, Sharon and Chuck,

   _____.
                                              1

   I just got an increase in my salary, and I'm just so excited. We have to go out and celebrate.

2. SHARON: _____.
                                              2

   Hey, I know a really good place downtown. I was just there last night.

3. CHUCK: Well, I'm really happy, Bette,

_____
3

4. BETTE: Well, then come on out with us.

5. SHARON: Yeah, let's go. Yeah.

6. CHUCK: But ...

_____,
4

and we have to work tomorrow.

7. SHARON: Oh, listen ...

8. BETTE: Oh, listen I only get it ... a salary raise once in ... how many years?

9. SHARON: That's right and you can

_____
5

10. CHUCK: I can ... how can I take tomorrow morning off?

11. SHARON: Well, just call in.

12. BETTE: Just don't show up.

13. SHARON: Yeah, It's easy. Hey,

_____,
6

you know ...

14. CHUCK: Well ...

15. SHARON: ... they have velvet walls, and the drinks are really good.

16. BETTE: A really good band, Chuck, a really good band ...

17. CHUCK: Bette, Bette, there's ... there's a little thing about money ...

18. BETTE: ... we can dance all night!

19. CHUCK: ... a little thing about money with me too. I didn't get an increase in my salary.

20. SHARON: Well, that's all right.

_____.
7

She'll pay.

21. BETTE: Yeah, it's my treat.

22. SHARON: Yeah, That's okay. And about work, you know, uh, call in ...

_____
8

so far this year.

23. CHUCK: Mmm. That's true. But also there's another small problem.

_____ ,
                                 9

an important phone call tonight.

24. BETTE: Ooooh ...

25. SHARON: Ooooh, really?

26. CHUCK: Yeah.

27. SHARON: No. Not important enough to miss the celebration.

28. BETTE: Not tonight. If it's so important,

_____ .
                                 10

29. SHARON: That's right ... yeah.

30. CHUCK: Hmm.

31. SHARON: And ... come on, let's go.

32. CHUCK: Where ...

33. SHARON: Okay?

34. CHUCK: _____ ?
                                 11

35. SHARON: You know, downtown, uh, the, the street ...

36. BETTE: It's right on the corner.

37. CHUCK: _____ ,
                                 12

and maybe I can meet you later.

38. SHARON: Oh, noooo ...

39. BETTE: Noooo chance ...

40. SHARON: Uh-uh.

41. BETTE: Noooo chance.

42. SHARON: Because if you meet us later, you won't come and you know it.

43. CHUCK: Sure I will. I'll come.

44. SHARON: Uh-uh.

TAKING PART

Choose two partners and act out the situations below.

Situation One

Background: One person has just gotten a raise and invites his/her friends to go out and celebrate.

SPEAKER #1 You are very excited because you just got a raise. Invite your friends to go out and celebrate with you tonight. Tell them that the evening will be your treat.

SPEAKER #2 You are very enthusiastic about going out and celebrating your friend's raise. However, another friend is reluctant to go. Try to convince him/her to accompany you.

SPEAKER #3 You are happy about your friend's raise, but you don't want to go out and celebrate. You are afraid you might offend your friends by saying no directly. Make excuses why you can't go out.

Situation Two

Background: Three friends are discussing going to a beach house for the weekend.

SPEAKER #1 You have a small house near the beach. Invite your friends to spend this weekend at your beach house with you. Tell them that you can guarantee a wonderful weekend of sun, fun and comfort.

SPEAKER #2 You are very enthusiastic about spending the weekend at your friend's beach house. However, another friend is reluctant to go. Try to convince him/her to accompany you.

SPEAKER #3 You are very pleased that your friends have included you in their weekend plans. But you are a little embarrassed because you've gained some weight over the winter and cannot get into your swimsuit. And besides, you don't really like the beach. You don't want to offend your friends by simply saying "no," and you are afraid that they will think you are silly if you explain the real reasons. Make excuses why you can't go.

SPEAKING OUT

Read the discussion topics below and choose one to talk or write about.

1. In the United States recent studies show that people are not going to work as often as they should. The rate of absenteeism seems to be increasing. Is this true in your native country? What does this show about people's attitudes toward work?

2. Describe what you like to do most for relaxation. What kinds of things do you prefer to do alone? What kinds of things do you prefer to do with a group?

3. In the dramatization one person said he didn't want to go out because he was expecting a phone call. This might not have been true; it might have been an excuse not to go out. Have you ever done something similar? Why? What excuses do you sometimes use when you don't want to do something?

4. Choose your own discussion topic related to the dramatization.

GOOD TEACHERS

MONOLOG

TUNING IN

Study these words if they are new to you.

1. *discipline:* controlled behavior
2. *strict:* insistent on good behavior
3. *labor:* work
4. *oratory:* the art of public speaking
5. *rubber-stamp:* use a piece of rubber with raised letters to print something again and again
6. *pay off:* have good results

SUMMING UP

Read these questions before you hear the recording. Then listen to the recording and answer the questions.

1. What did Gary's good teachers demand from their students?

2. What did the sign over his teacher's door mean?

3. What did she do and also require her students to do?

4. According to Gary, what kinds of teachers do students sometimes dislike?

5. When do students realize the importance of good teachers?

RETELLING

State the ideas in the monolog in your own words. You can use the phrases below as a guide.

The teachers that Gary respects the most _____

_____ .

He remembers one teacher who _____ .

_____

_____ .

She always _____

and demanded _____ .

One time _____ but _____

_____ .

Gary thinks that teachers who demand the most _____

_____ .

FILLING IN

Listen to the recording and fill in the blanks.

A good teacher is many things to many people, I think. I suppose everyone has _____
1

ideas about what a _____ teacher is. Uh, in my _____ experience I look back
2   3

_____ my old teachers, and _____ think the people that _____ respect the
4   5   6

most, and _____ think about the most _____ those that demanded the _____
7   8   9

discipline from their students.

_____ think of one teacher _____ particular that I had _____ high school. I
10   11   12

think _____ was a good teacher _____ she was a very _____ person. She just
13   14   15

tolerated _____ kind of nonsense at _____ in her classroom. I _____ very
16   17   18

vividly a sign _____, uh, her classroom door. It _____ a simple sign that _____,
19   20   21

"Laboratory—in this room _____ first five letters of _____ word are emphasized,
22   23

not _____ last seven." In other _____, I guess, labor for _____ was more
24   25   26

important than _____.
27

She always prepared _____ lectures and work for _____ day, and she demanded
                                    28   29

_____ her students do the _____. We got lots of _____ from her so there
        30   31   32

_____ a constant shuffling of _____ between her and the _____. One time
        33   34   35

when she _____ broken her arm, everybody _____ the class thought that _____
                  36   37   38

the homework load would _____ reduced, but it continued _____ the same, and
                                        39   40

she _____-stamped her name at _____ bottom of papers _____ show that she
            41   42   43

had _____ them.
            44

I think sometimes _____ who demand the most _____ perhaps liked the least,
                          45   46

_____ as time goes by, _____ discipline really seems to _____ off.
        47   48   49

SPEAKING OUT

Choose one of the topics below and make up your own monolog.

1. Talk about how your mother or father tried to teach discipline.
2. Discuss how teachers should discipline their students.
3. Describe a teacher that you will never forget.
4. Tell about any personal experience related to the topic of the monolog.

THE THIRD TIME THIS WEEK

DRAMATIZATION

TUNING IN

Study these words if they are new to you.

1. *trust:* believe in the honesty of someone
2. *behave:* act
3. *mess:* a state of disorder

TALKING IT OVER

Read the first three questions. Then listen to the dramatization and answer the questions.

1. What is the woman's relationship to the other people?
2. Are they having a friendly conversation or an argument?
3. Approximately how old do you think Gary and Chuck are?

Now read these questions. Then listen to the dramatization again and answer the questions.

4. What does the mother want to talk to her sons about?
5. What did she think happened to them?
6. Why is she angry?
7. What is Gary and Chuck's complaint about their mother?
8. What are her complaints about them?
9. What reasons do they give to explain their behavior the night before?

FOCUSING IN

Read these questions about the language the speakers use for specific purposes during the dramatization. Listen again, taking notes if you need to. Then discuss your answers to the questions.

1. The mother tells her sons they have been disobedient. In your own words, what does she say?

_____

2. One reason she is angry is that they did not call her. What does she say that shows she is angry?

_____

3. One of the boys tries to bargain with his mother to treat him like an adult. What does he say?

_____

4. The mother says she will treat her sons like adults on one condition. In your own words, what does she say?

_____

FILLING IN

Listen to the dramatization and fill in the missing words.

1. MOTHER: Oh, before you two go out,

_____
                                        1

2. GARY: What do you want, Mom?

3. MOTHER: Uh, Gary and Chuck, you know I told you that you had to be in by ten o'clock on week nights. And last night

_____
                                        2

4. GARY: But, Mom, I have a reason for that. We were out.

_____.
                                  3

5. MOTHER: Did you . . .

6. CHUCK: Yeah, there was a good reason. We tried.

7. MOTHER: Do you have a dime in your pocket to make a telephone call?

_____
                                  4

thinking that you were involved in some accident.

8. CHUCK: But . . .

9. GARY: But, Mom, you have to understand that we, we really, really tried . . .

10. CHUCK: But you have to . . . please . . .

11. MOTHER: And not . . . but this is the third time this week.

12. CHUCK: But . . . but . . . of course we will come home when you tell us to unless
            something

_____.
                                  5

You have to trust us, and you have to treat us like adults a little bit.

13. MOTHER: _____
                                  6

if you would act like adults.

14. GARY: Billy Ferguson's mother treats him like an adult.

15. MOTHER: Billy . . .

16. CHUCK: And if he doesn't come home exactly at the time,

_____
                                  7

because she treats him like an adult.

17. MOTHER: But he . . . I've talked to Mrs. Ferguson, and he usually . . .

18. CHUCK: Don't you think we're adults?

19. MOTHER: No, I don't think you're adults.

_____.
                                  8

You go out of here. Your room is a mess. You don't come home for dinner.

20. GARY: Mother . . .

21. CHUCK: I clean my room once a week. That's enough.

22. GARY: Mother, we try. Really we try to do what you want us to do.

23. MOTHER: Oh, Gary, I think that you try, but

_____,
9

actually. Really. You either, Chuck.

24. CHUCK: _____,
10

will you treat me like an adult?

25. MOTHER: If ... when you start acting like an adult, I will, of course.

26. GARY: Mom ... when we tried to call home, but

_____,
11

and we couldn't find any store open to get change. All I had was fifty cents.

27. CHUCK: And I didn't have any money.

28. MOTHER: Well, then, what were you doing out?

_____?
12

TAKING PART

Choose two partners and act out the situations below.

Situation One

Background: A parent is angry at his/her two children for arriving home late.

SPEAKER #1 You are a parent with two teenage children. They are supposed to be home by 10 o'clock on week nights. You are angry with them because they have been late three times this week. Explain why you are angry and tell them that they have to be more responsible.

SPEAKER #2 You are a teenager. You and your brother/sister were late because you couldn't get a bus and you didn't have any change to make a telephone call. Try to convince your mother/father that you were justified in being late.

SPEAKER #3 You are a teenager. You feel that you try very hard to be obedient, but last night it was impossible to get home on time. Try to convince your mother/father to trust you and your brother/sister and treat you like adults.

Situation Two

Background: Three students live in a large house together. One person does all the cooking, and the other two share the cleaning. They are discussing their household responsibilities.

SPEAKER #1 You are the cook. You are angry with your roommates because the house has been a mess for the past week and it is dirty too. Explain why you are angry and insist they share their responsibilities.

SPEAKER #2   You are supposed to clean the house every other week. This week was not your turn to clean so you let the house get messy and dirty. Convince your roommates that you are not responsible for the condition of the house.

SPEAKER #3   You were supposed to clean the house this week, but you had a busy week at school and with your social life. You have not found time to straighten the house, but you don't think it needs cleaning. Try to convince your roommates that you usually assume your responsibilities and that the house is not as dirty as they claim it is.

SPEAKING OUT

Read the discussion topics below and choose one to talk or write about.

1. Discuss how important it is to you to be on time. Does it depend on the situation? Does it depend on the country you are in? Discuss your ideas with your classmates.

2. The two teenagers in the dramatization say that Billy Ferguson's mother treats him like an adult. They use this as evidence that other parents treat their children differently from the way they are treated. Have you ever used a similar argument? Explain the circumstances and tell whether you were successful or not.

3. The mother in the dramatization complains that her sons' rooms are a mess and that they don't come home for dinner. What do/did your parents complain about the most? Why?

4. Choose your own discussion topic related to the dramatization.

UNIT 4

ADVERTISING

MONOLOG

TUNING IN

Study these words if they are new to you.

1. *market:* an area where there is a demand for goods
2. *compromise:* an agreement reached when each side yields to some of the demands of the other
3. *pressure:* influence

SUMMING UP

Read these questions before you hear the recording. Then listen to the recording and answer the questions.

1. Chuck gives three examples of ideas that come from advertising. What are two of them?

_____

2. According to Chuck, what do TV commercials tell us about certain products?

_____

3. What kind of work does his friend Karen do?

_____

4. What kinds of ideas does she get excited about?

_____

5. How concerned is Karen about the quality of the product that she's trying to sell?

_____

6. What does Chuck think of Karen's idea about advertising?

_____

RETELLING

State the ideas in the monolog in your own words. You can use the phrases below as a guide.

Chuck thinks it's amazing _____

_____.

Our ideas about _____

_____.

Television commercials tell us _____

_____.

He thinks it's unfortunate that _____.

His friend Karen _____

_____.

She feels excited when _____.

Chuck is worried that _____.

FILLING IN

Listen to the recording and fill in the blanks.

You know, it's just amazing how many of our ... ideas come from advertising ...

advertising in TV, advertising in magazines, on the radio.

It's a little bit _____ too, because our ideas _____ how we're supposed to

_____ and the kinds of _____ that we're supposed to _____ and the way that
   3   4   5

_____ supposed to look ... all _____ these things come from _____.
   6   7   8

Uh, television commercials tell us _____ if we don't use _____ right soap and
                                        9   10

shampoo _____ deodorant and cologne and _____ and then hair spray,
            11   12

_____ our friends won't go _____ with us. And unfortunately, _____ lot of
   13   14   15

people begin _____ believe this. And of _____ it's not true.
                16   17

Uh, markets _____ to be created, uh, yes, _____ I think that there _____ to
                18   19   20

be a little _____ of a compromise in _____ how much pressure is _____ on
              21   22   23

the public.

I _____ a friend, Karen, who _____ graduated from college with _____
   24   25   26

degree in, uh, television work. _____ very excited about her _____. It's very
                                              27   28

interesting. She _____ most excited, uh, when she _____ an idea that can
                      29   30

_____ used that she thinks _____ will convince people to _____ a certain product.
   31   32   33

And _____ seems to have very _____ idea about responsibility as _____
         34   35   36

the quality of the _____ that she's trying to _____. I wonder if this typi-...
                          37   38

_____ typical. Maybe it isn't _____, but if it is, _____ a little bit disturbing.
   39   40   41

SPEAKING OUT

Choose one of the topics below and make up your own monolog.

1. Choose a newspaper or magazine ad that you consider to be misleading. Explain your reasons.
2. Identify a specific brand of product that you always buy. Convince your class to buy that brand.
3. Explain why you agree or disagree with the idea that advertisers should be responsible for the quality of the products they try to sell.
4. Tell about any personal experience related to the topic of the monolog.

THE COMPETITION IS STIFF

DRAMATIZATION

TUNING IN

Study these words if they are new to you.

1. *discourage:* make someone lose interest or enthusiasm
2. *income:* money that a person receives regularly for work
3. *stiff:* difficult

TALKING IT OVER

Read the first three questions. Then listen to the dramatization and answer the questions.

1. Are the people friends, relatives or strangers?
2. Which person do you think is the youngest?
3. How would you describe the conversation? (polite or rude, calm or excited)

Now read these questions. Then listen to the dramatization again and answer the questions.

4. What is Chuck excited about?
5. Why do the women think Chuck should study something else?
6. What do they suggest for him to study?
7. What is Chuck confident that he can do?

FOCUSING IN

Read these questions about the language the speakers use for specific purposes during the dramatization. Listen again, taking notes if you need to. Then discuss your answers to the questions.

1. In your own words, how does Chuck express enthusiasm about his art course?

_____

2. One of the women suggests that Chuck study engineering. What does she say to try to convince him to change careers?

_____

3. The other woman suggests that he study commercial art. What does she say?

_____

4. Chuck responds negatively to their suggestions. In your own words, what does he say?

_____

FILLING IN

Listen to the dramatization and fill in the missing words.

1. CHUCK: Mom, I'm really excited about . . . about this, uh, art course I've gotten into now.

_____.
                                                    1

2. MOM: Well,

_____.
                                                    2

but I think you should be interested in other things too, you know.

3. SHARON: Uh, I don't want to discourage you, Chuck, but it's a difficult thing

_____.
                                                    3

Uh, the artist's life is not so easy, and maybe you should study something else so that you can earn a regular income.

4. CHUCK: Well, maybe before an artist's life wasn't so easy, but

_____
4

now. An artist can be himself and

_____
5

and paint the way he likes and not worry about so many other things.

5. MOM: Well, Chuck, that's true if you make it as an artist, but just think of how many other people are trying to become artists too. The competition is really stiff.

_____,
6

and then it takes many years . . .

6. SHARON: That's . . .

7. MOM: . . . before you're established, and before you're established, you just can't make any money.

8. CHUCK: _____.
7

9. SHARON: Well, I think maybe you should talk to some more artists. You know, I've been in the art community in New York for a long time, and, uh,

_____
8

who've had a very difficult life, and eventually they had to give it up, and then there was nothing they could do.

10. MOM: I mean

_____
9

or something, and you can . . .

11. CHUCK: Engineering!

12. MOM: . . . paint on weekends if you felt like it.

13. CHUCK: Paint on the . . . !

14. SHARON: Yeah.

15. MOM: Then, then you can always, if you sell,

_____.
10

then you can always give up the engineering.

16. CHUCK: I'm not at all interested in going into engineering. I want to paint.

17. MOM: Well,

_____
11

and a family.

18. CHUCK: I can support myself painting, I'm sure.

19. SHARON: Maybe you should study commercial art because that's a little bit easier.

20. CHUCK: I won't . . . I don't want to be commercial. I want to paint

_____
                                            12

21. SHARON: Well, of course you want to paint what you want to paint.

TAKING PART

Choose two partners and act out the situations below.

Situation One

Background: A teenager is discussing his/her career goals with a parent and a friend.

SPEAKER #1   You are an art student, and you want to become an artist. You are not interested in any other career. Express enthusiasm about your plans to your mother/father and friend and refuse to change careers.

SPEAKER #2   Your son/daughter has decided to become an artist. You are afraid that he/she will not be able to make enough money because the competition among artists is stiff. Try to encourage him/her to change career goals (for example, become an engineer) and paint on weekends.

SPEAKER #3   You are an artist. You know that an artist's life is very difficult and that it is not easy to earn a regular income. Politely suggest that your friend's son/daughter study something else, such as commercial art.

Situation Two

Background: A family is discussing the son's/daughter's future plans.

SPEAKER #1   You are in your last year of high school. You plan to go to college, but you want to get away from school for a while and travel first. You are extremely excited about a year on your own. Discuss your plans with your parents and refuse to consider starting college before you have had this experience.

SPEAKER #2   You are a parent. You don't want your son/daughter to travel because you are afraid that interrupting school will make it difficult for him/her to get into a good college. You are also worried about the dangers of a young person traveling alone. Try to encourage him/her to finish college before taking this trip.

SPEAKER #3   You are a parent. You didn't go to college and have always been proud of the fact that your child would get the education that you never had. You have been saving money since he/she was born for this purpose, and you want him/her to start right away. Try to discourage your son/daughter from traveling and suggest that the family take a trip together during the summer before college begins.

SPEAKING OUT

Read the discussion topics below and choose one to talk or write about.

1. Parents sometimes disapprove of the jobs or careers their children are interested in. Why do you think this happens? Has it ever happened in your family?

2. Are there any classes you are taking now that you like very much? Is there any special subject that you would like to study? Discuss your interests with your classmates.

3. Many people in the United States have become interested in living and working on farms. They think this kind of life is more satisfying than living in a city. Where do you live? Where would you like to live?

4. Choose your own discussion topic related to the dramatization.

CHANGES

MONOLOG

TUNING IN

Study these words if they are new to you.

1. *instances:* examples
2. *generation:* a period of time about 25 or 30 years
3. *amazement:* surprise

SUMMING UP

Read these questions before you hear the recording. Then listen to the recording and answer the questions.

1. According to Sharon, what is the main difference between life today and life many years ago?

_____

2. When was Sharon's friend born?

_____

3. What does Sharon mean when she says her friend is a "living history book"?

_____

4. What are some of the experiences her friend gets excited talking about?

_____

RETELLING

State the ideas in the monolog in your own words. You can use the phrases below as a guide.

Changes happen very quickly today. For Sharon it's hard to imagine _____

_____.

A friend of hers was born _____.

She is able to talk about _____

_____.

Her friend remembers _____

_____

_____.

In Sharon's opinion we've _____

_____.

FILLING IN

Listen to the recording and fill in the blanks.

There're so many things going on in modern lives, and change happens so quickly. It's hard to imagine _____ time when things were _____ and you could really _____ each new thing come _____ your life and to _____ even the day or _____ year that those things _____. I know that today, _____ example, there are many _____ of second and third _____ of things, of televisions _____ radios when some of _____ weren't even aware that _____ was a first generation.

_____ friend of mine was _____ at the end of _____ last century, and talking _____ her, I really get _____ sense of, of her _____ a living history book, _____ being able to, to _____ about the changes in _____ own life and to _____ that those changes were _____ the changes that society _____ going through.

She gets _____ excited, for example, when _____ talks about the first _____ she ever saw a _____ and even more excited _____ she saw herself in _____ picture that the photographer _____. She lived in a _____ town, and, at the _____ that she was very _____, there were no cars _____ trains in her city _____ all. As she grew _____, the cars and the _____ came in and she

_____ her first, her first _____ with a real sense _____ amazement that anyone
         40   41   42

could _____ so fast.
              43

    I guess _____ lost a little bit _____ getting away from this _____ of history.
                        44   45   46

Of course, _____ gained a lot too.
                   47

SPEAKING OUT

Choose one of the topics below and make up your own monolog.

1. Choose any invention and explain why you believe that the world would be better off *without* it.
2. Discuss what you consider to be an important scientific discovery of recent years.
3. Describe an interesting period in the history of your country.
4. Tell about any personal experience related to the topic of the monolog.

LET'S COMPROMISE

DRAMATIZATION

TUNING IN

Study these words if they are new to you.

1. *financial investment:* a way of using money to make more money
2. *stock:* part of the ownership of a business
3. *dividend:* part of the money made by a business that is divided among the owners
4. *compromise:* settle a disagreement by deciding on something acceptable to all sides
5. *wise:* showing good sense

TALKING IT OVER

Read the questions first. Then listen to the dramatization and answer the questions.

1. What do you think recently happened to the speakers?
2. What do you think their relationship is?
3. What are they trying to decide?

Now read these questions. Then listen to the dramatization again and answer the questions.

4. What does Chuck, the first speaker, want to do?
5. What does Bette want to do with the money? Do the others agree with her?
6. What does Gary want to do with the money?
7. How much money does Chuck want to spend immediately?

FOCUSING IN

Read these questions about the language the speakers use for specific purposes during the dramatization. Listen again, taking notes if you need to. Then discuss your answers to the questions.

1. Bette strongly disapproves of Chuck's idea. What does she say to him? How do you know she's annoyed?

_____

2. What does Chuck say to indicate that he doesn't think the cost of the stereo is important?

_____

3. What does Gary say to Bette *before* he disagrees with her? What do you think he is trying to do?

_____

4. Gary tries to settle their disagreement by suggesting they spend some money and save some money. How does he introduce his final suggestion?

_____

FILLING IN

Listen to the dramatization and fill in the missing words.

1. CHUCK: I just saw a new stereo the other day that's really big and beautiful and

_____.
                                        1

2. GARY: How much is it?

3. BETTE: Oh, now listen, just because you've got money

_____
                                        2

doesn't mean you should go out and spend it. You should put it in the bank.

4. CHUCK: Why not spend it?

5. GARY: Yeah, I agree. I agree, Bette, but let him talk and let him ... how, how much is it, Chuck?

6. CHUCK: _____.
                                         3
    We've got enough money for years and years and years and years. We can buy anything we want.

7. GARY: No ...

8. BETTE: Well, if you buy everything you want right away, you won't have any. Now,

    _____
                                         4

    and put it all in the bank or buy some real estate and diamonds ... make good financial investments and then we don't have to worry about money

    _____.
                                         5

9. GARY: Bette, I, I agree partially with you. I think, though, we should spend

    _____.
                                         6

    We can't put it all away. And in spending it ...

10. BETTE: Well, why not?

11. GARY: Well,

    _____.
                                         7

    In spending it, uh, we shouldn't spend it all on ourselves.

    _____
                                         8

    too.

12. CHUCK: Okay. I'm for that. We can help other people but spend it.

13. BETTE: Well, I don't know why. I, I think that we should take and put it all in the bank. Or invest it in real estate and diamonds and things.

14. GARY: Not all in the bank.

15. BETTE: Listen, if you invest it ...

16. CHUCK: Why do you want to put it all in the bank?

17. BETTE: ... Okay ... okay. Put it in the bank. Put it in stocks. Then you have dividends coming in every year ...

18. GARY: Listen ...

19. BETTE: Your money is always making money.

20. CHUCK: Oh, your stocks might fail. Your stocks might fail.

21. BETTE: Well, not if you make wise investments. Besides, diamonds and gold are always good investments. They'll always go up.

22. GARY: All right. All right. But listen.

_____
                                    9

so let's do ... let's compromise. Let's spend a little bit of it.

_____.
                                    10

23. BETTE: I know, but once you start spending ...

24. CHUCK: Okay, but let's start spending. And the stereo first.

25. BETTE: Once you start spending,

_____.
                                    11

26. CHUCK: And then a new car.

27. GARY: The original question—be quiet, Bette—how much is the stereo?

28. CHUCK: I don't remember,

_____.
                                    12

TAKING PART

Choose two partners and act out the situations below.

Situation One

Background: Three family members are discussing what to do with a large sum of money they have inherited.

SPEAKER #1   You are excited about having a lot of money because now you can buy anything you want. Suggest buying a large stereo and a new car.

SPEAKER #2   You are happy about the money you inherited, and you want to share it. Suggest saving some of the money, spending some of it on yourselves and spending some of it to help other people. Also try to find out how much the stereo costs.

SPEAKER #3   You are nervous about money. You feel very strongly about investing it for your future. You do not want to spend it on yourselves or on other people. Try to convince your relatives to invest the money.

Situation Two

Background: A husband and wife are talking with a real estate agent about buying a house.

SPEAKER #1   You and your spouse have been looking for a house for several months. The real estate agent has shown you a few houses today, but you haven't liked any of them. You are tired, and you want to stop looking for now. Suggest continuing your search another day.

SPEAKER #2   You and your spouse have looked at a few houses today. You know that the only way to find your "dream house" is to see as many houses as possible each day. Your spouse is tired, but try to convince him/her to continue looking today. Also try to find out more details about the last house you saw.

SPEAKER #3   You are a real estate agent. You have shown this couple many houses, and you want to make a sale. You sense that one of them liked the last house they saw. Try to convince them that it would be the best house for them and they don't need to look any further.

SPEAKING OUT

Read the discussion topics below and choose one to talk or write about.

1. In the dramatization the people are talking about what to do with money they have received. If you had a lot of money, what would you do with it? Can you think of any disadvantages of having a lot of money?

2. Many great people have lived without money. Why do you think some people choose to be poor? Would you choose to be poor? Why or why not?

3. One way to invest money is to start some kind of business or company. Can you think of a new business or company you would like to start? Explain why you think it would be profitable.

4. Choose your own discussion topic related to the dramatization.

CREDIT

MONOLOG

TUNING IN

Study these words if they are new to you.

1. *credit rating:* an evaluation which tells whether or not a person pays back money on time
2. *down payment:* part of the full price paid when something is bought
3. *finance:* provide money for
4. *a good credit risk:* a person who is known to pay back money on time
5. *ironic:* when a situation is the opposite of what you would expect

SUMMING UP

Read these questions before you hear the recording. Then listen to the recording and answer the questions.

1. According to Gary, what do we have to have to get along in society today?

2. What did Gary's brother want to do?

3. Why couldn't he borrow money?

4. What was he forced to do?

5. According to Gary, what is ironic about being able to borrow money?

RETELLING

State the ideas in the monolog in your own words. You can use the phrases below as a guide.

Gary says that having a credit rating _____

_____ .

His brother wanted to _____ .

He had enough money _____ , but

_____ .

He was forced to _____ .

Gary thinks it's ironic because _____

_____ .

FILLING IN

Listen to the recording and fill in the blanks.

Having a credit rating seems to be one of the most important things about living in the

society today. A good credit rating _____ important because in order _____ get
                                        1   2

money for something, _____ have to prove yourself, _____ yourself worthy of,
                               3   4

uh, having _____ money that you get _____ from the bank or _____ a savings
                5   6   7

and loan _____ what have you.
        8

Uh, it _____ ... this became obvious to _____ brother because he wanted
       9   10

_____ buy a house for _____ and his family after _____ for an awful long
  11   12   13

_____ , and he, uh, had enough _____ in the bank for _____ down payment
  14   15   16

on the _____ , but he couldn't get _____ loan for financing the _____ because he
     17   18   19

didn't have _____ cards. He believed in, uh, _____ cash for everything that
       20   21

_____ bought. So this in _____ forced him to open _____ accounts at various
  22   23   24

places _____ order to prove himself _____ good credit risk because _____
     25   26   27

you can't prove that _____ a good person to _____ money to, you're not
          28   29

_____ to be able to _____ any money. And it's _____ because you really have
  30   31   32

_____ owe money in order _____ borrow more money. So _____ is
    33   34   35

exactly what my _____ and his wife had _____ do, uh, and after a _____ of
                         36   37   38

years of actually _____ things on time, they _____ able to finance their _____.
                         39   40   41

SPEAKING OUT

Choose one of the topics below and make up your own monolog.

1. Talk about why you do or do not like to buy on credit.
2. Tell about a funny experience you once had with money.
3. Describe how you spend money during a one-week period.
4. Tell about any personal experience related to the topic of the monolog.

TWICE AS MUCH

DRAMATIZATION

TUNING IN

Study these words if they are new to you.

1. *make good money:* earn a high salary
2. *crab:* complain (*informal*)
3. *keep a record of:* write down
4. *household:* all the people living together in a house

TALKING IT OVER

Read the first three questions. Then listen to the dramatization and answer the questions.

1. How are the speakers related?
2. What are they discussing?
3. How would you describe the conversation? (calm or excited, friendly or angry)

Now read these questions. Then listen to the dramatization again and answer the questions.

4. What is the father's complaint?
5. What is the daughter's attitude toward money?
6. Who buys the groceries for the family? What does this person say about the cost of food?
7. What does the father want his wife and daughter to do? What do they think of his idea?
8. How much money does the mother want?

FOCUSING IN

Read these questions about the language the speakers use for specific purposes during the dramatization. Listen again, taking notes if you need to. Then discuss your answers to the questions.

1. The daughter sounds angry and speaks to her father disrespectfully. What are some of her comments?

_____

2. What does the father mean when he says, "...cut it out, both of you"?

_____

3. The father emphasizes that he expects his family to follow the new rule. What does he say?

_____

4. The mother complains that she needs more money. In your own words, what does she say?

_____

FILLING IN

Listen to the dramatization and fill in the missing words.

1. FATHER: _____
                                                    1

             about this money situation in our family.

2. BETTE: Oh, here he goes again.

3. MOTHER: But, Bette...

4. FATHER: I make good money, and you two spend it all.

5. BETTE: Look, Dad, I

             _____.
                                                    2

             You make so much money, you don't know how to spend it. I don't see what you crab about...

3
---

it makes.

6. MOTHER: But Bette, you know, the prices have

4

You don't buy the food for this family, and I do. And I know how much things are.

7. FATHER: All right, now just cut it out, both of you. I want to make a new rule in the, our house. I want . . .

8. BETTE: Oh, rules, rules . . . schmules!

9. FATHER:

5
---

of everything that you buy.

10. BETTE: Oh, I'm not going to do that.

11. MOTHER: Oh, we can't do that.

12. FATHER: No, I'm insisting on it.

6
---

anymore.

13. MOTHER: You're not throwing your . . .

14. BETTE: But you're not throwing your money away. What would you do with it anyway?

7
---

15. FATHER: I give both of you money every . . .

16. BETTE: What are you going to do? When you die you can't take it with you.

17. FATHER: I know. I know.

18. MOTHER: And you don't know either how much prices have increased. You don't give me

---
8
---

19. FATHER: I . . .

20. MOTHER: I have to buy groceries every month and you don't give me half enough. That's right. And I think that

---
9
---

you should start buying the groceries.

21. FATHER: Now who is the head of this household, you or me?

22. MOTHER: You are, and if you're worried about the money, then you should ... buy the groceries.

23. BETTE: And why don't you make more money

   _____
                                             10

   it?

24. FATHER: That is your job ... as the wife of ...

25. BETTE: Oh, boy!

26. MOTHER: It might have been, but if you were giving me enough money,

   _____.
                                             11

27. FATHER: _____?
                                             12

28. MOTHER: At least twice as much. Have you looked at the prices recently?

29. FATHER: You can't have twice as much money.

TAKING PART

Choose two partners and act out the situations below.

Situation One

Background: Three family members are discussing the budget for the household.

SPEAKER #1   You support your family, and you are angry because they spend so much money. Insist that they keep a record of everything that they buy.

SPEAKER #2   You are a student. You don't understand why your family is worried about money. Tell them that you think you have more than enough money and refuse to keep a record of everything you buy.

SPEAKER #3   You buy the groceries for the family, and you know how much prices have increased. You don't think that you waste any money. Explain that you need twice as much money to buy groceries and refuse to keep a record of everything you buy.

Situation Two

Background: Three neighbors in an apartment building are arguing in the hallway at 3 a.m. on a weekday.

SPEAKER #1   You are a light sleeper. You have not been able to sleep because your neighbor is having a party. He/she has refused to turn down the record player, and you are very angry. Go to the apartment and insist that the record player be turned down. Threaten to call the police.

SPEAKER #2 You are having a party in your apartment. You don't understand why your neighbor is so angry. You have already turned down the record player. It doesn't sound loud in your apartment. Tell him/her you think the complaint is unreasonable and refuse to turn down the music any more.

SPEAKER #3 You have two neighbors who are always arguing. You know how they act every time there is a party. Explain that their arguing keeps you awake more than the party. Insist that they come to an agreement or you will complain to the manager about both of them.

SPEAKING OUT

Read the discussion topics below and choose one to talk or write about.

1. Do you think a conversation like the one in the dramatization could occur between a husband and wife in your country? Why or why not?

2. Comparison shopping means going to many stores and looking at the same article to decide which one to buy. Do you think comparison shopping is worthwhile? Give examples to explain your point of view.

3. People in some countries go grocery shopping every day; in other countries they only go once a week. Why do you think this is true? How often do you or your family shop?

4. Choose your own discussion topic related to the dramatization.

UNIT 7

TOURISM

MONOLOG

TUNING IN

Study these words if they are new to you.

1. *tourism:* the travel business
2. *abroad:* to another country
3. *better off:* in an improved condition or situation
4. *on your own:* alone; without help

SUMMING UP

Read these questions before you hear the recording. Then listen to the recording and answer the questions.

1. According to Chuck, what do tour companies tell us we can learn from traveling?

_____

2. Why does Chuck think his friends were fortunate?

_____

3. What happened to the other members of the tour group?

_____

4. What reason does Chuck give for people not going out on their own?

_____

5. In his opinion, what would happen if tourists mixed more with local people?

_____

RETELLING

State the ideas in the monolog in your own words. You can use the phrases below as a guide.

According to Chuck, tourism is really a big business. It involves _____

_____.

Tour companies tell us _____

_____.

Chuck's friends went _____

with a tour group. Fortunately, _____

_____.

Other members of the tour group, however, _____

_____.

Chuck says he understands why _____

_____.

But he thinks _____

_____.

FILLING IN

Listen to the recording and fill in the blanks.

Boy, tourism is really a big business these days. It's amazing. It involves _____,
1
transportation, restaurants, shops, thousands _____ people. The tour companies
2
_____ telling us what a _____ thing it is . . . about _____ much we can
3   4   5
learn _____ people and customs, but _____ I wonder if this _____ really true.
6   7   8
Uh, a couple _____ I know went abroad, uh, _____ summer. They traveled with
9   10
_____ tour group. It's interesting _____ compare their experiences with
11   12
_____ of the experiences of _____ people in the same _____ group. Uh,
13   14   15
my friends, fortunately, _____ some . . . some acquaintances, or _____, actually,
16   17
along the route _____ their tour. In some _____ the cities they were _____,
18   19   20

they knew some of _____ 21 ... they knew some local _____ 22 . Uh, so that when they

_____ 23 to different places, uh, they _____ 24 go out with some _____ 25 the local

people and _____ 26 could eat some of _____ 27 local food and maybe _____ 28

some of the local _____ 29 .

Uh, other members of the _____ 30 group, however, never got _____ 31 of the group

at _____ 32 . Uh, they . . . they never went _____ 33 and did a thing _____ 34 their own.

Uh, of course _____ 35 tour company leaves it _____ 36 much up to the . . .

_____ 37 to whatever they _____ 38 .

Uh, I understand why people _____ 39 go out on their _____ 40 because of language

problems _____ 41 being a little bit _____ 42 . But it seems to _____ 43 that, uh, the

more tourists _____ 44 mix with local people, uh, _____ 45 better off everyone is.

_____ 46 tour companies emphasized that, _____ 47 really would learn about _____ 48

people and other customs.

SPEAKING OUT

Choose one of the topics below and make up your own monolog.

1. Describe an interesting trip you once took.
2. Describe some ways of meeting new people when you are in a foreign country.
3. Tell about a time when misunderstanding what someone said created a problem for you.
4. Tell about any personal experience related to the topic in the monolog.

LET'S MAKE A DEAL

DRAMATIZATION

TUNING IN

Study these words if they are new to you.

1. *sushi:* Japanese food made with raw fish and rice
2. *standardized:* without variation
3. *broiled:* (food) cooked directly under strong heat
4. *folks:* people (*informal*)

TALKING IT OVER

Read the first three questions. Then listen to the dramatization and answer the questions.

1. Are the speakers friends or strangers?
2. What are they discussing?
3. In what country does the conversation take place?

Now read these questions. Then listen to the dramatization again and answer the questions.

4. Where does Sharon, the first speaker, want to go tonight?
5. How does Bette feel about Sharon's suggestion?
6. Where does Chuck want to go? Why?
7. What do Bette and Sharon think of Chuck's idea?
8. What does Bette suggest as a compromise?

FOCUSING IN

Read these questions about the language the speakers use for specific purposes during the dramatization. Listen again, taking notes if you need to. Then discuss your answers to the questions.

1. Sharon invites her friends to go out for dinner with her. In your own words, what does she say?

   _____

2. What does Chuck mean when he says, "I don't know about sushi"?

   _____

3. What does Bette mean when she says, "Oh, Chuck, really"?

   _____

4. Chuck suggests to Sharon that they go out without Bette. In your own words, what does he say?

   _____

5. Bette suggests that they stay in the hotel. In your own words, what does she say?

   _____

6. What kind of "deal" do you think Chuck was going to make?

   _____

FILLING IN

Listen to the dramatization and fill in the missing words.

1. SHARON: Hey, you know, the hotel clerk told me about a great sushi restaurant.

   _____.
   1

   Do you want to go out for dinner tonight?

2. BETTE: Oh, I'm really tired.

   _____.
   2

going anyplace tonight.

3. SHARON: But it's not very far.

_____
3

4. CHUCK: Well, Bette,

_____
4

I'm really hungry too. But I don't know about sushi. I, I heard there's a . . . a McDonald's or two McDonald's in Kyoto that I'd really like to try.

5. BETTE: Oh, Chuck, really!

6. SHARON: Chuck . . .

7. BETTE: You come all the way to Japan to eat hamburgers! You can get them anytime at home.

8. CHUCK: But . . . but . . . but we . . . we could find out if they're, you know, the same quality and . . .

9. SHARON: Oh, of course they're going to be the same quality . . .

10. BETTE: Well, I really don't care.

11. SHARON: . . . they're standardized, but . . .

12. CHUCK: But you don't know that they're standar- . . .

13. SHARON: . . . sushi is good for you.

14. CHUCK: But I'd much rather have hamburgers.

15. BETTE: Well, I'm . . . sorry.

_____
5

And I have to admit that raw fish just doesn't really appeal to me.

16. CHUCK: So, let's go and eat hamburgers at McDonald's.

17. SHARON: But raw fish is . . . you don't have to eat raw fish. I mean you can eat . . .

18. BETTE: What do you mean?

19. SHARON: Well, there's a kind . . .

20. BETTE: That's all that comes in sushi.

21. SHARON: Nooo!

_____
6

th- . . . using a k- . . . kind of fish that's broiled.

_____
7

22. CHUCK: But, Sharon, you know Bette has a sensitive stomach.

23. SHARON: But I really don't think McDonald's hamburgers are the solution.

24. CHUCK: Of course, she's used to that kind of food.

25. BETTE: Why don't you folks go out and

   _____?
                                        8

   I just want to go home and go to bed.

26. CHUCK: Let's go out . . .

27. SHARON: Oh, no.

28. CHUCK: Sharon, you and I can go out, and

   _____.
                                        9

   How's that?

29. SHARON: But I don't . . .

30. BETTE: I . . .

31. SHARON: . . . think we should eat hamburgers. I really think it's . . . the experience of
            coming to Japan should include eating Japanese food.

32. BETTE: Well, I agree with you, Sharon.

33. CHUCK: Let's make a deal. Tonight . . .

34. BETTE: I know what. Listen, there's a . . .

35. CHUCK: . . . tonight, hamburgers.

36. BETTE: . . . real nice Japanese restaurant

   _____.
                                        10

   Why don't we just go down there and have a bite to eat?

37. SHARON: The hotel . . .

   _____!
                                        11

TAKING PART

Choose two partners and act out the situations below.

Situation One

Background: Three American tourists are in Japan, talking about where to have dinner.

SPEAKER #1 You feel that eating Japanese food should be a part of your experience visiting
            the country. Recommend a sushi restaurant and try to convince your friends
            to go there with you.

SPEAKER #2   You would like to have Japanese food for dinner, but you're too tired to leave the hotel. Suggest having dinner at the Japanese restaurant in the hotel.

SPEAKER #3   You would like to eat hamburgers for dinner. Try to convince your friends to compromise with you by having hamburgers tonight and Japanese food another night.

Situation Two

Background: Three co-workers are trying to decide how they can save money commuting to and from work. All three drive their own cars to work now.

SPEAKER #1   You think that forming a car pool with your co-workers is the best way to save money. You also think it will help reduce air pollution. Recommend that the three of you take turns driving to work. Try to convince them that it is the most economical solution.

SPEAKER #2   You think that forming a car pool with your co-workers is a good idea, but you just bought a big new car. It uses a lot of gas, but you like driving it every day. Suggest that you drive your co-workers to work every day and that they share your car expenses with you.

SPEAKER #3   You think that taking the bus to work is the only way to save money. You also think it's the best way to help reduce air pollution. Try to convince your co-workers to compromise by taking the bus three or four times a week and driving the other days.

SPEAKING OUT

Read the discussion topics below and choose one to talk or write about.

1. How important to you is the food, service and atmosphere of a restaurant? Compare the restaurants in your native country with restaurants in other countries you have visited.

2. Do you agree with the saying, "When in Rome, do as the Romans do"?

3. What makes people laugh? Do you mind if people laugh at you when you try to do new things? Why or why not?

4. Choose your own discussion topic related to the recorded dramatization.

QUALITY OF GOODS

MONOLOG

TUNING IN

Study these words if they are new to you.

1. *merchandise:* things for sale
2. *workmanship:* skill in making things
3. *assembly line:* a line of workers and machines in which each person has a particular job to do to make a product
4. *on sale:* offered for sale at a reduced price

SUMMING UP

Read these questions before you hear the recording. Then listen to the recording and answer the questions.

1. According to Chuck, why did people take pride in workmanship in the past?

2. How are most things made now?

3. What is Chuck's definition of "built-in obsolescence"?

4. How long had Chuck's friend Mary had her toaster before it broke?

5. Why wouldn't the people at the store take the toaster back and refund Mary's money?

6. What advice does Chuck offer?

RETELLING

State the ideas in the monolog in your own words. You can use the phrases below as a guide.

Chuck says that in the past _____

_____ .

But now _____

_____ .

Things have to be replaced because _____ .

For example, his friend Mary bought _____ .

After a couple of months _____

_____

_____ .

She took it back _____ ,

but _____ .

So she had to _____ .

Chuck thinks we should _____ .

FILLING IN

Listen to the recording and fill in the blanks.

Do you ever feel the quality of the merchandise we buy these days isn't as good as it ought to be?

In the past, when _____ were made by hand, _____ seems there was a

            1   2

_____ of pride in individual _____ ... people were really proud _____ the

  3   4   5

kinds of things _____ made.

              6

But, of course, _____ individuals don't make things. _____ of the things that

                7   8

_____ use are made on _____ lines and ... one person _____ has a very

  9   10   11

small _____ in putting something together _____ there isn't any pride

      12   13

_____ workmanship anymore.

  14

We _____ the term "built-in _____" a lot these days, uh, _____ means
that things are _____ to fall apart after _____ given period of time _____ they
have to be _____.

A good example of _____ is a friend of _____, uh, Mary. Mary, last summer,
_____ a toaster. She bought _____ on sale. She used _____, I guess, pretty
often, _____ she only had it _____ couple of months when, uh, _____ the
plastic base on _____ toaster cracked wide open, _____ at the same time _____
heating element in the _____ burned out.

She took _____ back to the store _____, uh, she was told in _____ store
that since she _____ bought it on sale, _____ wouldn't take it back, _____
they wouldn't give her _____ money back. So the _____ thing Mary could do
_____ to buy a new _____.

Uh, I'm sure Mary's a _____ more careful when she _____ things now, and that's
_____ what we all have _____ be.

SPEAKING OUT

Choose one of the topics below and make up your own monolog.

1. Describe something you have done or made that you feel proud of.
2. Describe something you own that you don't think you could replace.
3. Discuss several ways that consumers could force manufacturers to make better quality products.
4. Tell about any personal experience related to the topic of the monolog.

IT DOESN'T WORK

DRAMATIZATION

TUNING IN

Study these words if they are new to you.

1. *refund:* money given back for something returned
2. *insulting:* saying or doing something to offend (someone)
3. *impertinent:* not polite or respectful

TALKING IT OVER

Read the first three questions. Then listen to the dramatization and answer the questions.

1. Where does the conversation take place?
2. What is the woman trying to do?
3. How would you describe the conversation? (calm or excited, friendly or angry)

Now read these questions. Then listen to the dramatization again and answer the questions.

4. What is the store policy?
5. Why doesn't the customer want to have the machine repaired? What does she demand instead?
6. What are the store clerks trying to find out?
7. Why does the customer feel insulted?
8. According to the clerk, what is the woman doing wrong?

FOCUSING IN

Read these questions about the language the speakers use for specific purposes during the dramatization. Listen again, taking notes if you need to. Then discuss your answers to the questions.

1. The customer begins with a request. What does she say?

_____

2. The store clerk explains the store policy and offers to have the machine repaired. In your own words, what does he say?

_____

3. The customer refuses the store clerk's offer. What does she say that shows her frustration?

_____

4. The customer demands to speak to the store manager. What does she say?

_____

5. One of the clerks tries to get the customer to calm down. In your own words, what does he say?

_____

FILLING IN

Listen to the dramatization and fill in the missing words.

1. CUSTOMER: Uh,

    _____
    1

    tape recorder and get a cash refund.

2. CLERK: Just what ... is the problem, ma'am?

3. CUSTOMER: It ... doesn't work.

4. MANAGER: _____,
    2

    but it's the store policy

    _____
    3

but ... of course, we will be happy to repair the machine for you.

5. CUSTOMER: I'm sorry, but this is the third time in six months that I've had to

_____.
4

Now this is just ridiculous.

6. CLERK: Now ...

7. MANAGER: But we will repair it free of charge.

8. CUSTOMER: I don't want it repaired. I want ... I just want my money back.

9. CLERK: Ma'am, uh,

_____
5

with the tape recorder?

10. CUSTOMER: I don't know. I don't know how to ... repair tape recorders. If

_____.
6

11. MANAGER: But

_____
7

is quite qualified to do that sort of thing.

12. CUSTOMER: Well, then,

_____?
8

13. CLERK: Well,

_____?
9

14. CUSTOMER: It doesn't work. Try it yourself.

15. MANAGER: Have you dropped it?

16. CUSTOMER: Of course not!

17. MANAGER: Left it in the rain?

18. CUSTOMER: Of ...

_____
10

young man? I think you're absolutely impertinent.

19. CLERK: Now, madam ... madam, calm down.

20. CUSTOMER: Let me speak to the manager.

21. CLERK: C- ... calm down.

22. CUSTOMER: I want to speak to the manager.

23. MANAGER: I am the manger.

24. CUSTOMER: I demand to speak ...

25. MANAGER: I am the manager.

26. CUSTOMER: You are not.

27. MANAGER: I am the manager. And it's our policy that we ...

28. CUSTOMER: You are n- ... I want ... I want to speak to the store manager, please.

29. CLERK: Madam, could you just explain ...

30. MANAGER: The store manager isn't here.

31. CLERK: .... calm down, please. Don't ... don't get upset. I ...

32. CUSTOMER: Here it is. Try and work it yourself.

33. CLERK: Well, now,

_____?
                                    11

34. CUSTOMER: None of them! Look at this.

35. MANAGER: _____,
                                    12

madam.

TAKING PART

Choose two partners and act out the situations below.

Situation One

Background: A customer in a department store wants to return a tape recorder that is not working.

SPEAKER #1 You are the customer. You are angry because this is the third time in six months that your tape recorder has had to be repaired. Demand your money back.

SPEAKER #2 You are a store clerk waiting on an angry customer who demands a cash refund for a broken tape recorder. Try to calm the customer down and find out what is wrong with the machine.

SPEAKER #3 You are the store manager. You overhear a customer's demand for a cash refund for a broken tape recorder. Explain the store's policy not to refund money and offer to have the machine repaired.

Situation Two

Background: A customer in a furniture store is complaining about the inconvenience the store has caused him/her and is demanding a refund.

SPEAKER #1   You are the customer. You have wasted three days at home waiting for the delivery of your new sofa. Every time you called about it, you were told that the sofa would be delivered immediately, but it never arrived. You are so angry that you don't want the sofa anymore. Demand your money back.

SPEAKER #2   You are a salesperson. Your customer is very angry because his/her sofa has not been delivered. Try to calm the customer down and offer to find out what the problem is.

SPEAKER #3   You are the store manager. An angry customer demands a cash refund for an undelivered sofa, but the store does not give refunds. Explain the store's policy and offer to have the sofa delivered immediately.

SPEAKING OUT

Read the discussion topics below and choose one to talk or write about.

1. Have you ever had trouble taking something back to a store? Why? Discuss the store's policy and how you felt about it.

2. In the dramatization the customer was angry and raised her voice. Have you ever been in a public place and overheard an argument? Describe the situation and how it made you feel.

3. Choose your own discussion topic related to the dramatization.

UNIT 9

EAVESDROPPING

MONOLOG

TUNING IN

Study these words if they are new to you.

1. *eavesdropping:* listening secretly to other people's conversations
2. *hobby:* an activity done for pleasure during a person's free time
3. *compliment:* say something nice about or to someone

SUMMING UP

Read these questions before you hear the recording. Then listen to the recording and answer the questions.

1. What is Sharon's hobby?

_____

2. Where does she suggest listening to conversations?

_____

3. Where was she eavesdropping recently?

_____

4. What kind of game were the two people playing?

_____

5. What were they talking about as they were playing the game?

_____

64

RETELLING

State the ideas in the monolog in your own words. You can use the phrases below as a guide.

One of Sharon's hobbies is _____

_____.

She likes to listen to conversations in _____

_____.

Recently she _____

_____.

Their conversation was amusing because _____

_____

_____.

As they played the game, the two people _____

_____

_____.

She thought it was _____.

FILLING IN

Listen to the recording and fill in the blanks.

Conversations are really kind of interesting. I guess it's a _____ hobby of mine
                                                                    1
_____ listen to conversations that _____ can hear in public. _____ amazing
   2   3   4
how different the _____ or the tone or _____ content of different conversations
                    5   6
_____ be and to listen _____ the, the differences in _____ language that people
   7   8   9
use _____ they speak to different _____.
      10   11

If you're ever in _____ bookstore or a _____ store, it's interesting to _____
                    12   13   14
how the same salesperson _____ to different people. There're _____ interesting
                            15   16
places to listen _____ conversations too, I think, _____ one place that I've
                    17   18

_____ is on bus trips. _____ often talk to each _____ as if no one _____
_19_   _20_   _21_   _22_

were there. I guess _____ think that other people _____ hear their
                     _23_   _24_

conversations.

Recently _____ was on a bus, _____ I was listening to _____ conversation
          _25_   _26_   _27_

of two people _____ me. I can't really _____ I was listening, I _____. It would
               _28_   _29_   _30_

have been _____ not to hear it. _____ was amusing to listen _____ the two
           _31_   _32_   _33_

people, though, _____ they were playing a _____ of language, uh, word game
                 _34_   _35_

_____ states and state capitals. _____ person would say the _____ of the
 _36_   _37_   _38_

state, and _____ other person would say _____ name of the capital.
            _39_   _40_

_____ sounds like a kind _____ simple game that doesn't _____ much
 _41_   _42_   _43_

language and you _____ think that it would _____ very much conversation, but
                  _44_   _45_

_____ this wasn't the case _____ as they were playing _____ game, they
 _46_   _47_   _48_

continued to _____ one another and to _____ about how much they _____
              _49_   _50_   _51_

about history and how _____ of the other things _____ they could or couldn't
                       _52_   _53_

_____ about those places from _____ trips or from their _____.
 _54_   _55_   _56_

It was really kind _____ fun to listen to _____.
                    _57_   _58_

SPEAKING OUT

Choose one of the topics below and make up your own monolog.

1. Explain what you consider to be the qualities of a good conversationalist (a person who spends a lot of time in conversation).
2. Tell about a personal experience that involved eavesdropping.
3. Identify your favorite topic of conversation and explain why you like to talk about it.
4. Tell about any personal experience related to the topic of the monolog.

ONE MORE RULE
DRAMATIZATION

TUNING IN

Study these words if they are new to you.

1. *associate:* co-worker
2. *crony:* a friend or companion (*informal*)

TALKING IT OVER

Read the first three questions. Then listen to the dramatization and answer the questions.

1. Are the speakers friends, relatives or strangers?
2. What are they discussing?
3. How would you describe the conversation? (calm or excited, friendly or angry, polite or rude)

Now read these questions. Then listen to the dramatization again and answer the questions.

4. Why does the father complain about his family using the telephone?
5. Why does Bette need to use the telephone?
6. What is the new rule?
7. Why does the mother object to the rule?
8. What does Bette think of it?

FOCUSING IN

Read these questions about the language the speakers use for specific purposes during the dramatization. Listen again, taking notes if you need to. Then discuss your answers to the questions.

1. The father tells his family that he wants to talk to them. What does he say to get their attention?

_____

2. The mother begins by suggesting that Bette uses the phone too much. What does she say? How does she soften what she says?

_____

3. Betty complains about the telephone rules. In your own words, what does she say?

_____

4. The father threatens his family about breaking the rule. What does he say?

_____

FILLING IN

Listen to the dramatization and fill in the missing words.

1. FATHER: I need to talk to ... the two of you a little while

   _____.
                                        1

   Recently ...

2. BETTE: Oh, here he goes again.

3. FATHER: ... recently I've been getting a lot of phone calls from my office and from business associates, and

   _____.
                                        2

   Uh ...

4. MOTHER: I think, Bette, that that's your problem, isn't it?

_____.
3

when I want to talk on the phone too.

5. BETTE: What do you mean?

_____
4

to talk to friends.

_____
5

have another phone in this house.

6. FATHER: _____,
6

Bette. You see your friends every day at school...

7. BETTE: What do you mean? I do not...

8. FATHER: Every day after school.

9. BETTE: _____.
7

And you make so many stupid rules. You can't talk. You cannot talk on the
phone after nine o'clock. You can only talk for three minutes. Can't do this.
Can't do that.

10. FATHER: Well, we're going to make ... we're going to make

_____.
8

From now on, anybody that talks on the telephone, whether it's your mother or
me or you, Bette, five minutes and then stop.

11. BETTE: Oh, boy! Oh, boy!

12. MOTHER: Five minutes! Look...

13. FATHER: Five minutes is long enough.

14. MOTHER: ...you're out every day...

15. BETTE: And I'm the only one who'll have to follow that rule. That's not fair.

16. MOTHER: And you're out every day.

_____
9

I don't see my friends every day the way you do.

17. FATHER: _____,
10

you talk for hours with those old cronies.

18. MOTHER: I don't talk for hours.

19. BETTE: And what am I going to do when my boy friends call, anyway?

20. FATHER: Talk to them at school.

21. BETTE: That's the ... I don't get a chance to talk to them at school.

11

that I do.

22. FATHER: Well, five minutes. And if you break that rule ...

23. BETTE: That's not enough. That's not enough time.

24. FATHER: ... I'll take the telephone out.

25. BETTE: _____.
12

26. MOTHER: Well ...

27. FATHER: Well, that's his problem.

TAKING PART

Choose two partners and act out the situations below.

Situation One

Background: Three family members are discussing the use of the telephone at home.

SPEAKER #1 You are the head of the household and receive a lot of business calls at home. Insist that your family limit their calls to five minutes and threaten to take the phone out if they don't.

SPEAKER #2 You spend a lot of time at home and enjoy using the telephone. Explain your position and refuse to put a time limit on your calls.

SPEAKER #3 You are a student and often use the phone after school to talk to your friends. Complain about the phone rules and explain why you think they are unfair.

Situation Two

Background: Three people are discussing a mistake in change in a drugstore.

SPEAKER #1 You are a customer. You have just paid for items totaling $3.85. The clerk put your bill in the register and gave you $1.15 as your change for a five dollar bill. Insist that you gave the clerk a ten dollar bill. Threaten to call the manager if you are not given the correct change.

SPEAKER #2 You are a new clerk in a drugstore. You have had a difficult time finding a job and are very eager to keep this one. A customer claims he/she gave you a ten dollar bill and you have only given change for $5.00. You have already put the bill in the cash register, but you are sure it was only $5.00. Explain your position. Refuse to call the manager and suggest counting all the money in the cash register instead.

SPEAKER #3 You have been waiting in line in a drugstore for a long time. The person in front of you is having an argument with the clerk. Complain about the delay to the clerk and suggest that they end the dispute by calling the manager.

SPEAKING OUT

Read the discussion topics below and choose one to talk or write about.

1. In the dramatization the mother said the telephone was important to her because she stayed home all day. Do you think there are problems created by women staying home? How do women spend most of their time in your native country? Discuss the advantages and disadvantages of women staying home.

2. Do you think parents should make rules for a household to follow? Why or why not? Give specific examples of the rules you had to follow when you were growing up. Describe how you felt about them.

3. How important is using the phone in your life? Could you or would you like to live in a place without phones? Why or why not?

4. Choose your own discussion topic related to the dramatization.

WORKING

MONOLOG

TUNING IN

Study these words if they are new to you.

1. *contribute:* add to
2. *establish:* set up

SUMMING UP

Read these questions before you hear the recording. Then listen to the recording and answer the questions.

1. In Sharon's opinion, what is one of the most important things about working?

_____

2. Where did Sharon's sister Cindy work for a long time?

_____

3. Why did she decide to leave her job?

_____

4. What has made Cindy have a new opinion about the place of work in her life?

_____

RETELLING

State the ideas in the monolog in your own words. You can use the phrases below as a guide.

In Sharon's opinion, one of the most important things _____

_____

Her sister Cindy _____ .

_____ .

As she became more experienced, _____ .

_____ .

_____ .

But after a while, _____ .

_____ .

So she took a chance _____ .

_____ .

Now her sister feels _____ .

_____ .

FILLING IN

Listen to the recording and fill in the blanks.

Work is, uh, an important part of any person's life, and I think one of the most important things when you think about working is doing something that both makes you happy and gives you some sense of, of contributing to the richness of your own life.

My sister Cindy worked _____(1)_____ an office for quite _____(2)_____ long time, and she _____(3)_____ really very good at _____(4)_____ work. She was able _____(5)_____ do all of the _____(6)_____ of typical things that _____(7)_____ do in an office _____(8)_____ terms of typing and _____(9)_____ and, and managing the _____(10)_____ to the office. And _____(11)_____ she worked and became _____(12)_____ experienced, she was also _____(13)_____ a lot of responsibility _____(14)_____ planning the work of _____(15)_____ office and for making _____(16)_____ about the direction that _____(17)_____ work would go. But _____(18)_____ a while she really _____(19)_____ tired of being inside _____(20)_____ day. She didn't really _____(21)_____ sitting down and just _____(22)_____ at a desk, and _____(23)_____ though the work was _____(24)_____ enough, she felt that _____(25)_____ was, in the end, _____(26)_____ of boring. So she _____(27)_____ a chance on going _____(28)_____ to school, and she _____(29)_____ to become a trucker.

_____ a big truck isn't _____, but she became very _____ at it. Now she
   30   31   32

_____ feels that being outside _____ being able to establish _____ own
   33   34   35

schedule and being _____ mostly to herself for _____ work that she does
                       36   37

_____ given her an entirely _____, uh, opinion about the place _____ work in
   38   39   40

her own _____.
       41

SPEAKING OUT

Choose one of the topics below and make up your own monolog.

1. Explain why you decided upon your chosen career.
2. Discuss what you consider to be your major responsibilities at home, at work or at school.
3. Tell about a time when you took a chance.
4. Tell about any personal experience related to the topic of the monolog.

WHO'S MORE QUALIFIED?

DRAMATIZATION

TUNING IN

Study these words if they are new to you.

1. *nominate:* suggest someone (officially) for a position
2. *in the long run:* after a long period of time
3. *chauvinist:* someone unreasonably devoted to his/her sex, race or nation
4. *exception:* someone or something that is different

TALKING IT OVER

Read the first three questions. Then listen to the dramatization and answer the questions.

1. Are the speakers close friends, co-workers or strangers?
2. What are they discussing?
3. How would you describe the conversation? (calm or excited, polite or rude)

Now read these questions. Then listen to the dramatization again and answer the questions.

4. What does Sharon, the first speaker, think of Miss Yoshida's nomination?
5. Why is Bette pleased about the nomination?
6. What is Gary's opinion of Miss Yoshida's nomination? Why?
7. What is Bette's concern about the nomination?
8. What does Sharon try to convince them to do?

FOCUSING IN

Read these questions about the language the speakers use for specific purposes during the dramatization. Listen again, taking notes if you need to. Then discuss your answers to the questions.

1. Sharon is enthusiastic about Miss Yoshida's nomination. In your own words, how does she begin the conversation?

2. Bette initially disagrees with Gary, but then she says, "There's something to what Gary says ...." What does she mean?

3. Sharon tells Bette that she understands her point of view. How does Sharon express this?

4. How is this argument different from the arguments you heard in Unit 8, "It Doesn't Work" or Unit 9, "One More Rule"?

FILLING IN

Listen to the dramatization and fill in the missing words.

1. SHARON: Gee, don't you think it's really great that Miss Yoshida's been nominated to be
   _____?
   ₁

2. BETTE: Yes, I do. You know, Yoshida is s- ... so well-liked. She really gets along with people well.
   _____.
   ₂

3. SHARON: That's true. And I really think it's nice that it's a woman that's been nominated. You know women have had trouble for such a long time.

4. GARY: But in the long run

3

that a man be the head of the English department.

5. SHARON: Why?

6. BETTE: Why, Gary?

7. SHARON: What's so special about a man?

8. GARY: Because

4

9. SHARON: Oh, well, I don't think so.

10. BETTE: Well, I don't think that has anything to do with it. I mean,

---
5

as to ... who is more qualified.

11. SHARON: Right. And I th-...

12. GARY: Both,

6

13. SHARON: Well ... then ...

14. GARY: But I think men are basically, inherently stronger than women.

15. SHARON: Oh, Gary, don't be such a chauvinist.

16. GARY: No, I'm not being ...

17. SHARON: That's not true. Look at Eleanor Roosevelt, for example.

18. GARY: Well, she's an exception to the rule, I think.

19. SHARON: I think that she's just an exception because she was lucky enough to beat

---
7

20. GARY: Well, we have to look at this very, very ... uh ...

21. BETTE: Well, Sharon, there's, there's something to what Gary says in that

---
8

it may be putting Yoshida in a difficult position if she is made department head.

22. SHARON: That's true. But that's why

_____
                                    9

and not bring up false arguments . . .

23. GARY: No, no . . .

24. SHARON: . . . like men being stronger.

25. GARY: Situations are going to arise in the future

_____
                                    10

can control the situation.

26. SHARON: That's . . .

27. BETTE: Well, I'm just wondering how her fellow male colleagues, you know, in . . . in the
              university college are going to react to

_____
                                    11

28. GARY: That's a good point.

29. SHARON: That's a good point, and I think that since we all know she's qualified, that with
              our support

_____
                                    12

TAKING PART

Choose two partners and act out the situations below.

Situation One

Background: Three English teachers are discussing the new department chairperson at their
school.

SPEAKER #1 You are very happy that a woman is going to be chairperson of the department.
Express enthusiasm about the appointment and try to convince the other
teachers to support the woman.

SPEAKER #2 You think men are stronger than women. Try to convince the other teachers that
it is important to have a man as head of the department.

SPEAKER #3 You don't think it is important if the chairperson is male or female. But you feel
that a woman may have difficulty being accepted by the men in the
department. Express approval of the woman and concern for the problems
she may have in the position.

Situation Two

Background: A downtown company is considering moving to a new office in the suburbs. Three co-workers are discussing the move.

SPEAKER #1 You are very excited about the new office because it is larger and more modern than the office downtown. Express enthusiasm about the new location and try to convince your co-workers to appreciate it.

SPEAKER #2 You think the new office is too far from the city. You don't want to drive to the suburbs every day, and you're worried that business will decline because of the location. Try to convince your co-workers that a new location would be a mistake.

SPEAKER #3 You think that a new modern office would be nice, and you don't mind driving to the suburbs. But you are worried that being in the suburbs will hurt business. Express interest in the new office as well as concern for the location.

SPEAKING OUT

Read the discussion topics below and choose one to talk or write about.

1. Think of a famous person you admire and describe him/her to your classmates. Discuss the characteristics that make you admire the person.

2. The man in the dramatization said that men are stronger than women. Do you agree with him? Why or why not?

3. Choose your own discussion topic related to the dramatization.

ANSWERS

UNIT 1

Summing Up

1. We expect people to be dishonest.
2. because he still thinks there are honest people around
3. that the cashier had given him $10 – 15 more than he was supposed to have
4. He returned the money.
5. that there really are honest people around

Talking it Over

1. three
2. strangers
3. outside of a department store
4. a twenty dollar bill on the sidewalk
5. The wind blew it out of her hand.
6. when she tried to pay her bill in the department store
7. outside the store
8. determine who dropped the money

Focusing In

1. "I'm sorry but I think that's my money you've got."/"I'm sorry."
2. "No, it's my money. The wind just blew it out of my hand."/"I'm so sorry."
3. "Excuse me. What's going on here?"
4. "This is ridiculous!"/frustrated

UNIT 2

Summing Up

1. make decisions
2. They can make decisions quickly.
3. because their mother has given them a lot of responsibility at an early age
4. choose their own clothes
5. Their parents never let them decide anything.

Talking It Over

1. friends
2. They have jobs.
3. go out and celebrate
4. She just got a raise.
5. He has to work the next day, he has no money and he's expecting a phone call.
6. It has velvet walls, and the drinks and band are really good.
7. Bette will pay for everything.

Focusing In

1. "I'm so excited about my raise. I really want you to go out and celebrate with me!"
2. "I'm really happy that you got a raise, but ..."
3. He probably means he doesn't have enough money to go out.
4. "Why don't you go ahead, and I can meet you later."

UNIT 3

Summing Up

1. discipline
2. Working is more important than talking in the classroom.
3. prepare for each day's lesson
4. teachers who demand discipline
5. as time goes by

Talking It Over

1. She is their mother.
2. an argument
3. teenagers
4. about staying out too late
5. She thought they had been in an accident.
6. Last night was the third time they came home late this week, and they didn't call her.
7. She doesn't treat them like adults.
8. They don't clean their rooms; they don't come home for dinner.
9. They couldn't get a bus, and they didn't have any change to call.

Focusing In

1. "You're supposed to be home by ten o'clock, and this is the third time this week you've been late."
2. "Do you have a dime to make a telephone call?"
3. "If I clean my room two times a week, will you treat me like an adult?"
4. "I will treat you like adults when you start behaving like adults."

UNIT 4

Summing Up

1. how we're supposed to live; what clothes we're suposed to wear; the way we're supposed to look
2. If we don't use them, our friends won't go out with us.
3. advertising for television
4. ideas that convince people to buy certain products
5. not very concerned
6. He thinks it's disturbing.

Talking It Over

1. relatives (one woman could be a friend)
2. probably Chuck
3. polite and calm
4. his new art course
5. An artist's life is difficult, the competition is stiff, and it takes a long time to become established.
6. engineering or commercial art
7. support himself by painting

Focusing In

1. "I'm taking an art course that's so interesting. I'm really excited about it!"
2. "Why don't you go into engineering and paint on weekends? If you sell your paintings, then you can give up engineering."
3. "Maybe you should study commercial art because that's a little easier."
4. "I don't want to study engineering or commercial art at all. I want to be an artist, and that's what I'm going to be!"

UNIT 5

Summing Up

1. Change happens more quickly today.
2. at the end of the last century
3. The changes in her friend's life were the changes society was going through.
4. the first time she saw a camera and a photograph of herself; her first car and train rides

Talking It Over

1. They received a lot of money.
2. They're probably relatives.
3. what to do with the money
4. buy a stereo
5. invest it or put it in the bank; no
6. spend some of the money on themselves, help other people with some of it and save some of it
7. He doesn't know.

Focusing In

1. "Oh, now listen. Just because you've got money all of a sudden doesn't mean you should go out and spend it."/She stresses "Oh, now listen."
2. "Well, it doesn't matter."
3. "I agree partially with you."/be polite to her
4. "We've got the money, so let's compromise."

UNIT 6

Summing Up

1. a good credit rating
2. buy a house
3. He didn't have a credit rating.
4. open charge accounts
5. You have to owe money to borrow it.

Talking It Over

1. mother, father, daughter
2. spending money
3. excited and angry
4. His wife and daughter spend too much money.
5. Money should be spent.
6. the mother/Prices have doubled in the last year.
7. keep records of what they spend/They dislike the idea.
8. twice as much

Focusing In

1. "Here he goes again"; "I really think this is ridiculous"; "Rules, rules, schmules"; "You can't eat your money"; "When you die, you can't take it with you"; "Why don't you make more money if you're so worried about it?"
2. Stop arguing.
3. "I'm insisting on it. I'm not throwing my money away anymore."
4. "Have you looked at prices lately? You don't give me half enough money to buy groceries."

UNIT 7

Summing Up

1. We can learn about other people and customs.
2. They had some friends in the different places they traveled.
3. They never left the group to see things on their own.
4. because of fear and language problems
5. Everyone would learn about people and customs.

Talking It Over

1. friends
2. where to have dinner
3. Japan
4. to a sushi restaurant
5. She doesn't want to go out to eat, and sushi doesn't appeal to her.
6. to McDonald's for hamburgers/He doesn't want to eat sushi.
7. They don't think they should eat hamburgers in Japan; they should eat Japanese food.
8. She suggests that they eat in the Japanese restaurant in their hotel.

Focusing In

1. "Hey, I heard about a great sushi restaurant. Do you want to go there tonight?"
2. "I don't think I want to eat sushi."
3. "That's ridiculous." or "I can't believe you're serious."
4. "Sharon, why don't we go out and bring Bette some hamburgers?"
5. "How about having dinner in the Japanese restaurant in the hotel? It's real nice."
6. tonight hamburgers—tomorrow night Japanese food

UNIT 8

Summing Up

1. because things were made by hand
2. on assembly lines
3. Things are made to fall apart easily so they have to be replaced.
4. a couple of months
5. She had bought it on sale.
6. to be careful when you buy things

Talking It Over

1. a department store
2. return a tape recorder
3. The clerks are calm; the customer is excited and angry.
4. They don't refund money, but they will repair the machine.
5. She has had it repaired three times, and it still doesn't work./She wants her money back.
6. what's wrong with the tape recorder
7. because they ask her if she dropped the recorder or left it out in the rain
8. She's pressing the wrong button.

Focusing In

1. "I'd like to return this tape recorder and get a cash refund."
2. "I'm sorry, but we don't give refunds. We will be glad to repair the machine."
3. "Now that is just ridiculous."
4. "I want to speak to the store manager, please."
5. "Calm down, please. Don't get upset."

UNIT 9

Summing Up

1. listening to conversations in public
2. in a book or department store, on buses
3. on a bus
4. a word game about states and state capitals
5. They complimented each other on their knowledge of history and talked about how many things they remembered from trips.

Talking It Over

1. relatives
2. using the phone
3. excited, angry, rude
4. because his business associates try to call him and the line is always busy
5. to talk to friends
6. No one in the family can use the phone for more than five minutes at a time.
7. She says she doesn't get out of the house during the day, and the phone is her only enjoyment.
8. She thinks it's unfair.

Focusing In

1. "I needed to talk to the two of you."
2. "I think that's your problem, isn't it?"/She says "I think" and adds "isn't it?"
3. "You make so many rules. You can't talk after nine, you can only talk for three minutes."
4. "If you break the rule, I'll take the telephone out."

UNIT 10

Summing Up

1. doing something that makes you happy and contributes to the richness of your life
2. in an office
3. She didn't like being inside all day.
4. being outside, being able to establish her own schedule and being responsible for her own work

Talking It Over

1. co-workers
2. whether or not a woman should be head of the English department
3. calm and polite
4. She thinks it's great, especially because a woman has been nominated.
5. because she thinks Miss Yoshida is well-liked and gets along well with people
6. He thinks it would be better to have a man as head of the department./because he thinks men are stronger than women and situations may arise that only a man could handle
7. Miss Yoshida might have a difficult time because women aren't accepted in such positions.
8. support Miss Yoshida

Focusing In

1. "Isn't it great that Miss Yoshida's been nominated to be head of the department?"
2. Gary has made an important point.
3. She says "That's true" and "That's a good point."
4. It isn't an angry discussion; the speakers are polite to each other.

TAPESCRIPT

UNIT 1

Honesty (Monolog)

I read in the newspaper the other day that we tell between two hundred and three hundred lies every day. It makes me wonder if honesty is still important.

Uh, there're so many times when we just seem to expect people to be dishonest rather than be honest. We expect, uh, individuals to try to take advantage of other people whenever they can. And we sometimes expect politicians, uh, to . . . not always be honest in their dealings. And we even expect students, sometimes, to cheat on exams or, uh, do things to help their scores. I wonder if that's really fair to these people. Because I still think there're honest people.

The other day a very good friend of mine and I were in a restaurant. Uh, when the cashier gave him back, uh, his money, uh, after we got out of the restaurant, he realized that he had ten or fifteen dollars more than he was supposed to have. He didn't even hesitate at all. He went right back in and gave it back, and of course, the cashier was very happy.

But, uh, I was pleasantly surprised, because it means that there really are people running around who are honest.

That's My Money (Dramatization)

1. FIRST WOMAN: Uh, I'm sorry but I think that's my money you've got.

2. SECOND WOMAN: No, I just dropped it. I was walking into the store, and the wind was rather strong and blew it out of my hand. I'm sorry. You must've lost some money someplace else.

3. FIRST WOMAN: Uh, but, uh, I had forty dollars this morning, and I've only got twenty now, and I had it when I got out of the taxi. I just went inside the store.

4. SECOND WOMAN: Well, I'm . . . I'm sorry that you don't seem to be able to keep track of your money, but . . .

5. POLICEMAN: Excuse me. What's going on here?

6. SECOND WOMAN: I'm sorry. This lady thinks that this is her money, and I've just dropped it and picked it up, and if you'll talk to her, I'll just be on my way.

7. FIRST WOMAN: I know it's my money.

8. POLICEMAN: Uh . . .

9. FIRST WOMAN: I mean, I came out, and she . . . she had it in her hand. She's just picked it up.

10. POLICEMAN: Well, don't get excited. Let's just talk about it for a minute. You have the money. When did you pick up the money? Where did you find the money first?

11. SECOND WOMAN: Well, I didn't find the money. I just dropped it. I got out of the taxi, and I opened my wallet to pay the taxi driver, and the wind blew the twenty dollar bill onto the ground, and I just stooped to pick it up, and she saw the bill and thought that somebody had lost it and tried to get it first, but actually . . .

12. POLICEMAN: I see. I see.

13. FIRST WOMAN: But . . . (sigh)

14. POLICEMAN: What makes you think that was yours?

15. FIRST WOMAN: I had ... I had forty dollars in my pocketbook just a minute ago. I just went into the store, and when I tried to pay for something, I noticed that twenty dollars was gone, and I came out, and here ... here it was on the ground just as she started to pick it up.

16. POLICEMAN: Is it possible you could've dropped your money inside the department store?

17. FIRST WOMAN: I don't think so.

18. SECOND WOMAN: I think that you must have because I just ...

19. FIRST WOMAN: I mean, I found it on the sidewalk. I mean it was right there when she was trying to pick it up.

20. SECOND WOMAN: Actually it was my money that you found because the wind just blew it out of my purse when I tried to pay the taxi driver.

21. FIRST WOMAN: Oh, now really!

UNIT 2

Decision Making (Monolog)

It's amusing to me to watch some of my friends who can come to a decision right away, and then some others who can't. Some people can look at a menu, can pick up a menu and right away know what they're going to have for dinner that night. Then others will ponder and look at the thing and not be able to reach any kind of a decision for a long, long time without some help.

I was thinking about this when I was talking to my sister the other day, and I thought about her children, uh, how they come to decisions. It seems to me that for young children they come to decisions very quickly, and I was thinking about this, and I ... one of the reasons might be that she has given them a great deal of responsibility at a very young age. She has allowed them to make decisions on their own. She takes them shopping many times, and she allows them to choose clothes of their own liking, and I think in a way this teaches a great deal of responsibility. Uh, of course, they consult with her sometimes, but, uh, many times they're able to decide on something on their own, and I was thinking about my friends and how they were ... some of them were not able to make a decision on their own and maybe their parents didn't allow them to decide on something, decide on clothes.

Let's Go Out and Celebrate (Dramatization)

1. BETTE: Gee, Sharon and Chuck, you just have to go out. I just got an increase in my salary, and I'm just so excited. We have to go out and celebrate.

2. SHARON: That's a good idea. Hey, I know a really good place downtown. I was just there last night.

3. CHUCK: Well, I'm really happy, Bette, that you got an increase in salary.

4. BETTE: Well, then come on out with us.

5. SHARON: Yeah, let's go. Yeah.

6. CHUCK: But ... tomorrow is Tuesday, and we have to work tomorrow.

7. SHARON: Oh, listen ...

8. BETTE: Oh, listen I only get it ... a salary raise once in ... how many years?

9. SHARON: That's right and you can take tomorrow morning off.

10. CHUCK: I can ... how can I take tomorrow morning off?

11. SHARON: Well, just call in.

12. BETTE: Just don't show up.

13. SHARON: Yeah. It's easy. Hey, there's this really nice place, you know . . .

14. CHUCK: Well . . .

15. SHARON: . . . they have velvet walls, and the drinks are really good.

16. BETTE: A really good band, Chuck, a really good band . . .

17. CHUCK: Bette, Bette, there's . . . there's a little thing about money . . .

18. BETTE: . . . we can dance all night!

19. CHUCK: . . . a little thing about money with me too. I didn't get an increase in my salary.

20. SHARON: Well, that's all right. Bette got an increase. She'll pay.

21. BETTE: Yeah, it's my treat.

22. SHARON: Yeah. That's okay. And about work, you know, uh, call in . . . you haven't missed any work
              so far this year.

23. CHUCK: Mmm. That's true. But also there's another small problem. I'm expecting a phone call,
              an important phone call tonight.

24. BETTE: Oooh . . .

25. SHARON: Ooooh, really?

26. CHUCK: Yeah.

27. SHARON: No. Not important enough to miss the celebration.

28. BETTE: Not tonight. If it's so important, they'll call back later.

29. SHARON: That's right . . . yeah.

30. CHUCK: Hmm.

31. SHARON: And . . . come on, let's go.

32. CHUCK: Where . . .

33. SHARON: Okay?

34. CHUCK: Where is this place you're thinking about?

35. SHARON: You know, downtown, uh, the, the street . . .

36. BETTE: It's right on the corner.

37. CHUCK: Why don't you go ahead, and maybe I can meet you later.

38. SHARON: Oh, noooo . . .

39. BETTE: Noooo chance . . .

40. SHARON: Uh-uh.

41. BETTE: Noooo chance.

42. SHARON: Because if you meet us later, you won't come and you know it.

43. CHUCK: Sure I will. I'll come.

44. SHARON: Uh-uh.

UNIT 3

Good Teachers (Monolog)

A good teacher is many things to many people, I think. I suppose everyone has definite ideas about what a good teacher is. Uh, in my own experience I look back on my old teachers, and I think the people that I respect the most, and I think about the most are those that demanded the most discipline from their students.

I think of one teacher in particular that I had in high school. I think she was a good teacher because she was a very strict person. She just tolerated no kind of nonsense at all in her classroom. I remember very vividly a sign over, uh, her classroom door. It was a simple sign that said, "laboratory — in this room the first five letters of the word are emphasized, not the last seven." In other words, I guess, labor for her was more important than oratory.

She always prepared for her lectures and work for the day, and she demanded that her students do the same. We got lots of homework from her so there was a constant shuffling of papers between her and the students. One time when she had broken her arm, everybody in the class thought that maybe the homework load would be reduced, but it continued just the same, and she rubber-stamped her name at the bottom of the papers to show that she had read them.

I think sometimes teachers who demand the most are perhaps liked the least, but as time goes by, this discipline really seems to pay off.

The Third Time This Week (Dramatization)

1. MOTHER: Oh, before you two go out, I'd like to talk to you for just a minute.

2. GARY: What do you want, Mom?

3. MOTHER: Uh, Gary and Chuck, you know I told you that you had to be in by ten o'clock on week nights. And last night you were not home until eleven.

4. GARY: But, Mom, I have a reason for that. We were out. We couldn't get a bus back.

5. MOTHER: Did you . . .

6. CHUCK: Yeah, there was a good reason. We tried.

7. MOTHER: Do you have a dime in your pocket to make a telephone call? I sat here from ten to eleven thinking that you were involved in some accident.

8. CHUCK: But . . .

9. GARY: But, Mom, you have to understand that we, we really, really tried . . .

10. CHUCK: But you have to . . . please . . .

11. MOTHER: And not . . . but this is the third time this week.

12. CHUCK: But . . . but . . . of course we will come home when you tell us to unless something serious happens like last night. You have to trust us, and you have to treat us like adults a little bit.

13. MOTHER: I'd like to treat you like adults if you would act like adults.

14. GARY: Billy Ferguson's mother treats him like an adult.

15. MOTHER: Billy . . .

16. CHUCK: And if he doesn't come home exactly at the time she doesn't get so upset because she treats him like an adult.

17. MOTHER: But he . . . I've talked to Mrs. Ferguson, and he usually . . .

18. CHUCK: Don't you think we're adults?

19. MOTHER: No, I don't think you're adults. I don't think you behave like adults at all. You go out of here. Your room is a mess. You don't come home for dinner.

20. GARY: Mother ...

21. CHUCK: I clean my room once a week. That's enough.

22. GARY: Mother, we try. Really we try to do what you want us to do.

23. MOTHER: Oh, Gary, I think that you try, but I don't think you're trying hard enough, actually. Really. You either, Chuck.

24. CHUCK: If I clean my room two times a week, will you treat me like an adult?

25. MOTHER: If ... when you start acting like an adult, I will, of course.

26. GARY: Mom ... when we tried to call home, but we really didn't have any change, and we couldn't find any store open to get change. All I had was fifty cents.

27. CHUCK: And I didn't have any money.

28. MOTHER: Well, then, what were you doing out? Why weren't you home studying?

UNIT 4

Advertising (Monolog)

You know, it's just amazing how many of our ... ideas come from advertising, advertising in TV, advertising in magazines, on the radio.

It's a little bit frightening too, because our ideas about how we're supposed to live and the kind of clothing that we're supposed to wear and the way that we're supposed to look ... all of these things come from advertising.

Uh, television commercials tell us that if we don't use the right soap and shampoo and deodorant and cologne and toothpaste and then hair spray, that our friends won't go out with us. And unfortunately, a lot of people begin to believe this. And of course it's not true.

Uh, markets have to be created, uh, yes but I think that there has to be a little bit of a compromise in just how much pressure is put on the public.

I have a friend, Karen, who recently graduated from college with a degree in, uh, television work. Karen's very excited about her work. It's very interesting. She feels most excited, uh, when she has an idea that can be used that she thinks it will convince people to buy a certain product.

And Karen seems to have very little idea about responsibility as to the quality of the product that she's trying to sell. I wonder if this typi- is typical. Maybe it isn't really, but if it is, it's a little bit disturbing.

The Competition Is Stiff (Dramatization)

1. CHUCK: Mom, I'm reall excited about ... about this, uh, art course I've gotten into now. It's really interesting.

2. MOM: Well, I'm glad you enjoy it, but I think you should be interested in other things, too, you know.

3. SHARON: Uh, I don't want to discourage you, Chuck, but it's a difficult thing if you're interested in art. Uh, the artist's life is not so easy, and maybe you should study something else so that you can earn a regular income.

4. CHUCK: Well, maybe before an artist's life wasn't so easy, but I don't think it's so difficult now. An artist can be himself and do what he wants to and paint the way he likes and not worry about so many other things.

5. MOM: Well, Chuck, that's true if you make it as an artist, but just think of how many other people are trying to become artists, too. The competition is really stiff. And you have to be very good, and then it takes many years . . .

6. SHARON: That's . . .

7. MOM: . . . before you're established, and before you're established you just can't make any money.

8. CHUCK: But I think I can do it.

9. SHARON: Well, I think maybe you should talk to some more artists. You know, I've been in the art community in New York for a long time, and, uh, I have many, many friends who've had a very difficult life, and eventually they had to give it up, and then there was nothing they could do.

10. MOM: I mean why don't you go into engineering or something, and you can . . .

11. CHUCK: Engineering!

12. MOM: . . . paint on weekends if you felt like it.

13. CHUCK: Paint on the . . . !

14. SHARON: Yeah.

15. MOM: Then, then you can always, if you sell, if you can sell what you paint on **Sundays, then you** can always give up the engineering.

16. CHUCK: I'm not at all interested in going into engineering. I want to paint.

17. MOM: Well, at least you can support yourself and a family.

18. CHUCK: I can support myself painting, I'm sure.

19. SHARON: Maybe you should study commercial art because that's a little bit easier.

20. CHUCK: I won't . . . I don't want to be commercial. I want to paint what I want to paint.

21. SHARON: Well, of course you want to paint what you want to paint.

UNIT 5

Changes (Monolog)

There're so many things going on in modern lives, and change happens so quickly. It's hard to imagine a time when things were slower and you could really see each new thing come into your life and to remember even the day or the year that those things happened. I know that today, for example, there are many instances of second and third generations of things, of televisions or radios, when some of us weren't even aware that there was a first generation.

A friend of mine was born at the end of the last century, and talking to her, I really get a sense of, of her being a living history book, of being able to, to talk about the changes in her own life and to know that those changes were really the changes that society was going through.

She gets really excited, for example, when she talks about the first time she ever saw a camera, and even more excited when she saw herself in the picture that the photographer took. She lived in a small town, and, at the time that she was very young, there were no cars or trains in her city at all. As she grew up, the cars and the trains came in and she remembers her first, her first rides with a real sense of amazement that anyone could move so fast.

I guess we've lost a little bit in getting away from this period of history. Of course, we've gained a lot too.

Let's Compromise (Dramatization)

1. CHUCK: I just saw a new stereo the other day that's really big and beautiful and I think we ought to get it.

2. GARY: How much is it?

3. BETTE: Oh, now listen, just because you've got money all of a sudden doesn't mean you should go out and spend it. You should put it in the bank.

4. CHUCK: Why not spend it?

5. GARY: Yeah, I agree. I agree, Bette, but let him talk and let him ... how, how much is it, Chuck?

6. CHUCK: Well, it doesn't matter. We've got enough money for years and years and years and years. We can buy anything we want.

7. BETTE: No ...

8. BETTE: Well, if you buy everything you want right away, you won't have any. Now, I think we should take and put it all in the bank or buy some real estate and diamonds ... make good financial investments and then we don't have to worry about money for the rest of our lives.

9. GARY: Bette, I, I agree partially with you. I think, though, we should spend a little bit of it. We can't put it all away. And in spending it ...

10. BETTE: Well, why not?

11. GARY: Well, now listen to me. In spending it, uh, we shouldn't spend it all on ourselves. We should help other people too.

12. CHUCK: Okay. I'm for that. We can help other people but spend it.

13. BETTE: Well, I don't know why. I, I think that we should take and put it all in the bank. Or invest it in real estate and diamonds and things.

14. GARY: Not all in the bank.

15. BETTE: Listen, if you invest it ...

16. CHUCK: Why do you want to put it all in the bank?

17. BETTE: ... Okay ... okay. Put it in the bank. Put it in stocks. Then you have dividends coming in every year ...

18. GARY: Listen ...

19. BETTE: Your money is always making money.

20. CHUCK: Oh, your stocks might fail. Your stocks might fail.

21. BETTE: Well, not if you make wise investments. Besides, diamonds and gold are always good investments. They'll always go up.

22. GARY: All right. All right. But listen. We've got the money so let's do ... let's compromise. Let's spend a little bit of it. Let's save a little bit of it.

23. BETTE: I know, but once you start spending ...

24. CHUCK: Okay, but let's start spending. And the stereo first.

25. BETTE: Once you start spending, you never stop.

26. CHUCK: And then a new car.

27. GARY: The original question—be quiet, Bette—how much is the stereo?

28. CHUCK: I don't remember, but it doesn't really matter.

UNIT 6

Credit (Monolog)

Having a credit rating seems to be one of the most important things about living in the society today. A good credit rating is important because in order to get money for something, you have to prove yourself, prove yourself worthy of, uh, having this money that you get maybe from the bank or from a savings and loan or what have you.

Uh, it was . . . this became obvious to my brother because he wanted to buy a house for him and his family after renting for an awful long time, and he, uh, had enough money in the bank for the down payment on the house, but he couldn't get a loan for financing the house because he didn't have credit cards. He believed in, uh, paying cash for everything that he bought. So this in essence forced him to open charge accounts at various places in order to prove himself a good credit risk because if you can't prove that you're a good person to lend money to, you're not going to be able to get any money. And it's ironic because you really have to owe money in order to borrow more money. So this is exactly what my brother and his wife had to do, uh, and after a couple of years of actually buying things on time, they were able to finance their house.

Twice as Much (Dramatization)

1. FATHER: I'd like to talk to both of you about this money situation in our family.

2. BETTE: Oh, here he goes again.

3. MOTHER: But, Bette . . .

4. FATHER: I make good money, and you two spend it all.

5. BETTE: Look, Dad, I really think this is ridiculous. You make so much money, you don't know how to spend it. I don't see what you crab about . . . I don't see what difference it makes.

6. MOTHER: But Bette, you know, the prices have really gone up in the last year. You don't buy food for this family, and I do. And I know how much things are.

7. FATHER: All right, now just cut it out, both of you. I want to make a new rule in the, our house. I want . . .

8. BETTE: Oh, rules, rules . . . schmules!

9. FATHER: I want both of you to keep a record of everything that you buy.

10. BETTE: Oh, I'm not going to do that.

11. MOTHER: Oh, we can't do that.

12. FATHER: No, I'm insisting on it. I'm not throwing my money away anymore.

13. MOTHER: You're not throwing your . . .

14. BETTE: But you're not throwing your money away. What would you do with it anyway? You can't eat it.

15. FATHER: I give both of you money every . . .

16. BETTE: What are you going to do? When you die you can't take it with you.

17. FATHER: I know. I know.

18. MOTHER: And you don't know either how much prices have increased. You don't give me half enough to support this family.

19. FATHER: I . . .

20. MOTHER: I have to buy groceries every month, and you don't give me half enough. That's right. And I think that if you want people to keep records, you should start buying the groceries.

21. FATHER: Now who is the head of this household, you or me?

22. MOTHER: You are, and if you're worried about the money, then you should . . . buy the groceries.

23. BETTE: And why don't you make more money if you're so worried about it?

24. FATHER: That is your job . . . as the wife of . . .

25. BETTE: Oh, boy!

26. MOTHER: It might have been, but if you were giving me enough money, I'd be happy to do it.

27. FATHER: How much more money do you want?

28. MOTHER: At least twice as much. Have you looked at the prices recently?

29. FATHER: You can't have twice as much money.

UNIT 7

Tourism (Monolog)

Boy, tourism is really a big business these days. It's amazing. It involves hotels, transportation, restaurants, shops, thousands of people. The tour companies keep telling us what a good thing it is . . . about how much we can learn about people and customs, but sometimes I wonder if this is really true.

Uh, a couple that I know went abroad, uh, last summer. They traveled with a tour group. It's interesting to compare their experiences with some of the experiences of other people in the same tour group. Uh, my friends, fortunately, had some . . . some acquaintances, or friends, actually, along the route of their tour. In some of the cities they were going, they knew some of the . . . they knew some local people. Uh, so that when they got to different places, uh, they could go out with some of the local people and they could eat some of the local food and maybe see some of the local sights.

Uh, other members of the tour group, however, never got out of the group at all. Uh, they . . . they never went out and did a thing on their own. Uh, of course the tour company leaves it pretty much up to the . . . people to do whatever they want.

Uh, I understand why people wouldn't go out on their own because of language problems and being a little bit afraid. But it seems to me that, uh, the more tourists can mix with local people, uh, the better off everyone is. If tour companies emphasized that, everyone really would learn about other people and other customs.

Let's Make a Deal (Dramatization)

1. SHARON: Hey, you know, the hotel clerk told me about a great sushi restaurant. It's really close to the hotel. Do you want to go out for dinner tonight?

2. BETTE: Oh, I'm really tired. I really don't feel like going anyplace tonight.

3. SHARON: But it's not very far. It really is just down the street.

4. CHUCK: Well, Bette, we have to go out and eat. I'm really hungry too. But I don't know about sushi. I . . . I heard there's a . . . a McDonald's or two McDonald's in Kyoto that I'd really like to try.

5. BETTE: Oh, Chuck, really!

6. SHARON: Chuck . . .

7. BETTE: You come all the way to Japan to eat hamburgers! You can get them anytime at home.

8. CHUCK: But . . . but . . . but we . . . we could find out if they're, you know, the same quality and . . .

9. SHARON: Oh, of course they're going to be the same quality . . .

10. BETTE: Well, I really don't care.

11. SHARON: . . . they're standardized, but . . .

12. CHUCK: But you don't know that they're standar- . . .

13. SHARON: . . . sushi is good for you.

14. CHUCK: But I'd rather have some hamburgers.

15. BETTE: Well, I'm . . . sorry. I just really don't feel like it. And I have to admit that raw fish just doesn't really appeal to me.

16. CHUCK: So, let's go and eat hamburgers at McDonald's.

17. SHARON: But raw fish is . . . you don't have to eat raw fish. I mean you can eat . . .

18. BETTE: What do you mean?

19. SHARON: Well, there's a kind . . .

20. BETTE: That's all that comes in sushi.

21. SHARON: Nooo! There's a kind that's really nice th- . . . using a k- . . . kind of fish that's broiled. And that's really good.

22. CHUCK;   But, Sharon, you know Bette has a sensitive stomach.

23. CHUCK: But I really don't think McDonald's hamburgers are the solution.

24. CHUCK: Of course, she's used to that kind of food.

25. BETTE: Why don't you folks go out and eat whatever you want? I just want to go home and go to bed.

26. CHUCK: Let's go out . . .

27. SHARON: Oh, no.

28. CHUCK: Sharon, you and I can go out, and we'll bring Bette back some hamburgers. How's that?

29. SHARON: But I don't . . .

30. BETTE: I . . .

31. SHARON: . . . think we should eat hamburgers. I really think it's . . . the experience of coming to Japan should include eating Japanese food.

32. BETTE: Well, I agree with you, Sharon.

33. CHUCK: Let's make a deal. Tonight ...

34. BETTE: I know what. Listen, there's a ...

35. CHUCK: ... tonight, hamburgers.

36. BETTE: ... real nice Japanese restaurant down in the hotel lobby. Why don't we just go down there and have a bite to eat?

37. SHARON: The hotel ... they're too expensive!

UNIT 8

Quality of Goods (Monolog)

Do you ever feel the quality of the merchandise we buy these days isn't as good as it ought to be?

In the past, when things were made by hand, it seems there was a lot of pride in individual workmanship ... people were really proud of the kinds of things they made.

But, of course, now individuals don't make things. Most of the things that we use are made on assembly lines and ... one person only has a very small part in putting something together so there isn't any pride in workmanship anymore.

We hear the term "built-in obsolescence" a lot these days, uh, which means that things are made to fall apart after a given period of time so they have to be replaced.

A good example of this is a friend of mine, uh, Mary. Mary, last summer, bought a toaster. She bought it on sale. She used it, I guess, pretty often, but she only had it a couple of months when, uh, suddenly the plastic base on the toaster cracked wide open, and at the same time the heating element in the toaster burned out.

She took it back to the store, but, uh, she was told in the store that since she had bought it on sale, they wouldn't take it back, and they wouldn't give her her money back. So the only thing Mary could do was to buy a new toaster.

Uh, I'm sure Mary's a bit more careful when she buys things now, and that's probably what we all have to be.

It Doesn't Work (Dramatization)

1. CUSTOMER: Uh, I would like to return this tape recorder and get a cash refund.

2. CLERK: Just what ... is the problem, ma'am?

3. CUSTOMER: It ... doesn't work.

4. MANAGER: Well, I'm very sorry, madam, but it's the store policy we don't refund money, but ... of course, we will be happy to repair the machine for you.

5. CUSTOMER: I'm sorry, but this is the third time in six months that I've had to bring the thing back to be repaired. Now that is ridiculous.

6. CLERK: Now ...

7. MANAGER: But we will repair it free of charge.

8. CUSTOMER: I don't want it repaired. I want ... I just want my money back.

9. CLERK: Ma'am, uh, what seems to be the problem with the tape recorder?

10. CUSTOMER: I don't know. I don't know how to ... repair tape recorders. If I could do that I'd do it myself.

11. MANAGER: But our service department in our store is quite qualified to do that sort of thing.

12. CUSTOMER: Well, then, why haven't they fixed it?

13. CLERK: Well, can you explain what the trouble is?

14. CUSTOMER: It doesn't work. Try it yourself.

15. MANAGER: Have you dropped it?

16. CUSTOMER: Of course not!

17. MANAGER: Left it in the rain?

18. CUSTOMER: Of ... are you trying to be insulting young man? I think you're absolutely impertinent.

19. CLERK: Now, madam ... madam, calm down.

20. CUSTOMER: Let me speak to the manager.

21. CLERK: C— ... calm down.

22. CUSTOMER: I want to speak to the manager.

23. MANAGER: I am the manager.

24. CUSTOMER: I demand to speak ...

25. MANAGER: I am the manager.

26. CUSTOMER: You are not.

27. MANAGER: I am the manager. And it's our policy that we ...

28. CUSTOMER: You are n— ... I want to speak to the store manager, please.

29. CLERK: Madam, could you just explain ...

30. MANAGER: The store manager isn't here.

31. CLERK: ... calm down, please. Don't ... don't get upset. I ...

32. CUSTOMER: Here it is. Try and work it yourself.

33. CLERK: Well, now, which button does not work here?

34. CUSTOMER: None of them! Look at this.

35. MANAGER: You're pressing the wrong button, madam.

UNIT 9

Eavesdropping (Monolog)

Conversations are really kind of interesting. I guess it's a kind of hobby of mine to listen to conversations that I can hear in public. It's amazing how different the style or the tone or the content of different conversations can be and to listen to the, the differences in the language that people use when they speak to different people.

If you're ever in a book store or a department store, it's interesting to hear how the same salesperson talks to different people. There're other interesting places to listen to conversations too, I think, and one place that I've found is on bus trips. People often talk to each other as if no one else were there. I guess they think people can't hear their conversations.

Recently I was on a bus, and I was listening to a conversation of two people behind me. I can't really say I was listening. I guess it would have been hard not to hear it. It was amusing to listen to the two people, though, because they were playing a kind of language, uh, word game about states and state capitals. One person would say the name of the state, and the other person would say the name of the capital.

It sounds like a kind of simple game that doesn't involve much language, and you wouldn't think that it would involve very much conversation, but actually this wasn't the case because as they were playing this game, they continued to compliment one another and to talk about how much they knew about history and how many of the other things that they could or couldn't remember about those places from their trips or from their reading.

It was really kind of fun to listen to them.

One More Rule (Dramatization)

1. FATHER: I need to talk to ... the two of you a little while about the telephone. Recently ...

2. BETTE: Oh, here he goes again.

3. FATHER: ... recently I've been getting a lot of phone calls from my office and from business associates, and they always say the line is busy. Uh ...

4. MOTHER: I think Bette, that that's your problem, isn't it? I have noticed that the phone is busy when I want to talk on the phone too.

5. BETTE: What do you mean? That's the only time I get a chance to talk to friends. I don't see why we can't have another phone in this house.

6. FATHER: We don't need another phone, Bette. You see your friends every day at school ...

7. BETTE: What do you mean? I do not ...

8. FATHER: Every day after school.

9. BETTE: And we're always busy studying. And you make so many stupid rules. You can't talk. You cannot talk on the phone after nine o'clock. You can only talk for three minutes. Can't do this. Can't do that.

10. FATHER: Well, we're going to make ... we're going to make one more rule in this house. From now on anybody that talks on the telephone, whether it's your mother or me or you, Bette, five minutes and then stop.

11. BETTE: Oh, boy! Oh, boy!

12. MOTHER: Five minutes! Look ...

13. FATHER: Five minutes is long enough.

14. MOTHER: ... you're out every day ...

15. BETTE: And I'm the only one who'll have to follow that rule. That's not fair.

16. MOTHER: And you're out every day. That phone is my only enjoyment. I don't see my friends every day the way you do.

17. FATHER: When you go to the market, you talk for hours with those old cronies of ...

18. MOTHER: I don't talk for hours.

19. BETTE: And what am I going to do when my boy friends call, anyway?

20. FATHER: Talk to them at school.

21. BETTE: That's the ... I don't get a chance to talk them at school. Mike doesn't even go to the same school that I do.

22. FATHER: Well, five minutes. And if you break that rule, ...

23. BETTE: That's not enough. That's not enough time.

24. FATHER: ...I'll take the telephone out.

25. BETTE: It takes him five minutes to ask me for a date.

26. MOTHER: Well ...

27. FATHER: Well, that's his problem.

UNIT 10

Working (Monolog)

   Work is, uh, an important part of any person's life, and I think one of the most important things, when you think about working, is doing something that both makes you happy and gives you some sense of, of contributing to the richness of your own life.
   My sister Cindy worked in an office for quite a long time, and she was really very good at her work. She was able to do all of the sort of typical things that you do in an office in terms of typing and filing and, and managing the visitors to the office. And as she worked and became more experienced, she was also given a lot of responsibility for planning the work of the office, and for making decisions about the direction that the work would go. But after a while she really got tired of being inside all day. She didn't really like sitting down and just staying at a desk, and even though the work was varied enough, she felt that it was, in the end, kind of boring. So she took a chance on going back to school, and she learned to become a trucker.
   Driving a big truck isn't easy, but she became very good at it. Now she really feels that being outside and being able to establish her own schedule, and being responsible, mostly to herself, for the work that she does has given her an entirely new, uh, opinion about the place of work in her own life.

Who's More Qualified? (Dramatization)

1. SHARON: Gee, don't you think it's really great that Miss Yoshida's been nominated
             to be chairman of the department?

2. BETTE: Yes, I do. You know, Yoshida is s-, so well-liked. She really gets along with
             people well. She really knows how to handle them.

3. SHARON: That's true. And I really think it's nice that it's a woman that's been
             nominated. You know women have had trouble for such a long time.

4. GARY: But in the long run I think it's very important that a man be the head of the
             English department.

5. SHARON: Why?

6. BETTE: Why, Gary?

7. SHARON: What's so special about a man?

8. GARY: Because men are stronger than women.

9. SHARON: Oh, well, I don't think so.

10. BETTE: Well, I don't think that has anything to do with it. I mean, I think we should
             look at it as to ... who is more qualified.

11. SHARON: Right. And I th- ...

12. GARY: Both, both are equally qualified, I think.

13. SHARON: Well, then . . .

14. GARY: But I think men are basically, inherently stronger than women.

15. SHARON: Oh, Gary, don't be such a chauvinist.

16. GARY: No, I'm not being . . .

17. SHARON: That's not true. Look at Eleanor Roosevelt, for example.

18. GARY: Well, she's an exception to the rule, I think.

19. SHARON: I think that she's just an exception because she was lucky enough to beat
            the men at their own game.

20. GARY: Well, we have to look at this very, very, uh . . .

21. BETTE: Well, Sharon, there's, there's something to what Gary says in that because
            women aren't so accepted, it may be putting Yoshida in a difficult
            position if she is made department head.

22. SHARON: That's true. But that's why we have to support her even more and not
            bring up false arguments . . .

23. GARY: No, no . . .

24. SHARON: . . . like men being stronger.

25. GARY: Situations are going to arise in the future where a man and a man only can
            control the situation.

26. SHARON: That's . . .

27. BETTE: Well, I'm just wondering how her fellow male colleagues, you know, in . . .
            in the university college are going to react to a woman as department
            head.

28. GARY: That's a good point.

29. SHARON: That's a good point, and I think that since we all know she's qualified, that
            with our support that she can do it.